Is

Allah

God?

by Frans J.L. Zegers

Unless otherwise identified, Scripture quotations are from the King James Version of the Bible and the New King James Version of the Bible.

The quotations from the Koran are from the Koran-translation by N.J. Dawood (marked D), published by Penguin Classics, 1990, and the Koran interpretation by Arthur J. Arberry (marked A), published by Oxford University Press, 1991.

I have replaced God in these editions with the originally used name Allah. Because Mohammed does not speak of God but of Allah. The reason the modern editions of these books have replaced Allah with God is a political reason, and therefore objectionable from the view of truth and grammar! I motivate this within the pages of this book.

www.thevoiceofgodtoallnations.com

ISBN 978-1-4092-0122-9
Printed by Lulu.com

II

CONTENTS

Introduction   V

Chapter One   Allah has no son   1
Chapter Two   Jesus Christ is God   5
Chapter Three   The way Allah is worshipped   11
Chapter Four   Jerusalem or Mecca   17
Chapter Five   God fulfils His Word, the Bible   25
Chapter Six   The Name Allah   28
Chapter Seven   The Personality of Allah   36
Chapter Eight   Islamic Society - Kingdom of God   47
Chapter Nine   Allah changes people into apes & swine   67
Chapter Ten   Revelation of God compared to Allah   68
Chapter Eleven   Experiencing God compared to Allah   71
Chapter Twelve   Summery   75
Chapter Thirteen   Conclusion   81
Chapter Fourteen   Attention   86
Chapter Fifteen   The Gospel Of Jesus Christ Unto Salvation 90
Chapter Sixteen   Same Words – Different Meaning   108
Appendix   Links for More Information on the Internet 112

INTRODUCTION

In 1954 American Christians organised a conference in the little Lebanese mountain village of Bahamdun in which some 40 Christians and an equal number of Sunnite muslim spiritual leaders met.

These religious muslim leaders had agreed with this conference on certain conditions. The first that it would be attended by men only. The most important condition was that the motto of the conference would be: "We believe in the same God, the One, the Almighty, Creator of all the visible, the Judge at the end of human history."

For many Christians this motto was hard to swallow but they compromised and agreed for the sake of a meeting. The Dutch D. v.d. Meulen* , who replaced the invited Dr. H. Kraemer reports of this conference in the AO '78 booklet no. 1708 "*De Islam vroeger en nu.*" ("Islam, past and present.") The conference was organised by American Christians and sponsored by American great-industrials led by the Coca Cola company. All expenses including the week long stay in the luxury hotel and the flight tickets were paid for all the participants. (This became public when the books were opened after the Egyptian-Islamic press had printed the accusation that the money for the 'Bahumdun-convocation' was Jewish-Zionist.)

The Bahamdun conference was the first of its kind. Upon D. v.d. Meulen's return the Dutch Bible Society, the only commonly recognised ecumenical centre organised a meeting to discuss central points of criticism within the churches. For a pro- and contra-discussion had arisen within the church press. One central point of criticism was the motto of the conference " *We believe in one and the same God.*" D. v.d. Meulen writes, "*The result, of this meeting in Amsterdam too, also was a better understanding of what had taken place and a lesson for the right attitude for mission activities towards islam from now on. No longer:' Listen, muslim, I have something to tell you!' No, I listen to what you have to say. Then certainly the question will arise: 'and what then do you believe?' Beginning with listening, that is the new discovery for Christian missions to islam.*"

V

Not only is the latter remark one of utter naïveté as time has also proven since then. It is in clearly in conflict with Jesus' command to make all peoples His disciples, teaching them to observe all He had commanded His first disciples.

The statement reveals the humanistic infiltration and ecumenical brainwashing and the pride of those so called academics. It shows total ignorance, denial and setting aside of the Truth, of Jesus Christ, of God, of His Word, and also of the nature of islam and of the spirit islam. In 1955 another similar meeting of 'Christians' and muslims as organised. In 1956 Jerusalem, the holy city of muslims and Christians, was attempted as the meeting-place, but because of the unrest between Jews and muslims, this hope had to be abandoned at the last moment, and again Bahamdun was chosen. After that not much of it was heard again. But the World Council of Churches took up this example and continued it, more deeply and with 'more expertise'. A separate department was formed for the study and exercise of what was to be called "*the dialogue between christianity and islam.*" This has been going on with much financial support etc. for almost 40 years now. The results have even infiltrated our societies.

In our media, for example, and in revisions of existing versions of the Koran, and in new versions of the Koran, "Allah" nowadays is most often translated as "God". This implies that they are the same. Even the Koran itself says in one verse that Allah and God are one: "*Be courteous when you argue with the People of the Book, except with those among them who do evil. Say: 'We believe in that which is revealed to us and which was revealed to you. Our Allah and your God is one. To him we surrender ourselves.'*" (Sura 29:46 D) (This verse is from the time that Mohammed still sought to be recognised and accepted as a prophet by Jews and Christians.)

It is of utmost importance to establish whether they are the same or not.

My motivation for writing this book is that I love the Truth, Jesus Christ, and I hate all deception. Especially because by it's very nature, it deceives people. Why is there deception? Why does deception exist? By nature all deception is inspired by satan, because satan "*is a liar and the father of it.*" (John 8:44) That is why all people who live in

VI

deception are in bondage to satan, who is also called the devil! And when people's lives are in bondage to deception, it not only robs them of this life, but also of eternal life! **Deception is the devil's tool to lead people into eternal damnation!** So called 'enlightened' man does not even believe in the existence of the devil; he thinks he is so smart; but he does not know that he is deceived by the very one he denies the existence of: satan! What a fool 'enlightened' man is! By the truth and revelation of God I expose all deception that God has me expose, so that it may be seen in the face, and dealt with. Deception is not abstract. Deception is a spiritual person with a real face: satan, also called the devil!

When I expose the deception, I do not leave the people in a vacuum, like many communists found themselves in after the collapse of communism. That's a dangerous state to be in; vacuums by nature seek to be filled, and satan has plenty of other deceptions he wants to fill a person's vacuum with. Therefore if a person does not want to be deceived again, he must, by his deliberate choice, have his vacuum filled with Jesus Christ and His Word. My motive for this book therefore are the words of Jesus Christ in John 8:31,31, and 36: "*If you* (believers in Jesus Christ) *abide in My word, you are My disciples indeed. And you shall know the truth, and the truth shall make you free. Therefore if the Son makes you free, you shall be free indeed.*" I expose the deception, and at the same time I present the truth, so that those who live in the deception may know the truth and may be made free by the truth!

I am aware that to those who live in deception, no matter it's name, especially if that is the way they were raised in, this is painful. However, it is more painful to be eternally damned because of it. Therefore, like a doctor I diagnose the cancer of deception, which is a malignant cancer. The good news is that it can be removed in Jesus Christ, but in Him alone! So, because there is hope, I do not hesitate to tell the person in deception the true nature of the cancerous deception. Because I know that if the person heeds the words of this book, he too may have the cancerous deception removed from him, and be healed and receive the life of Jesus Christ, which is even eternal life! That is why, even when I realise the painful process this must be to the muslim, I do not hesitate to present him his diagnosis. If I would not do this, to avoid satan's possible backlashes through those belonging to him, those in deception would rightly accuse me of knowing the truth that could set them free, but not telling them. That would be the humanistic idea of love; but it is not love at all! That would really be hatred! To know the truth but to deny it to those who are going to eternal damnation by the deception they live in. Like leaving a drowning man to drown when I have the means to save him. So called 'enlightened' man may ask: "What is the truth?" Like deception is a spiritual person: satan, the devil; Truth also is a Person: Jesus Christ! For Jesus said: "*I am the way, the truth, and the life. No man comes to the Father except through Me.*" (John 14: 6) Jesus Christ did not say He is "a" truth, like the New-Agers want us to believe. No Jesus Christ is "THE" Truth, exclusively!

Muslims, are you willing to carefully consider my presentation? It is of vital importance to you that you do! I am not your enemy! I am an enemy to deception, to the devil. If you consider and carefully heed the truths presented in this book, you will know for yourself that I am not your enemy, and never was your enemy!

And think about it, muslims, why would you be afraid of this book? Why would you be afraid to read this book, or any true Christian book? If you believe that Islam is the true religion, how could any book be able to get you away from it? If your faith is so strong and if your religion is the true religion, no book will be able to get you away from it. But you will be able to better deal with Christianity! That is also why South-African Islamic apologist Ahmed Deedat encourages muslims to purchase and read the Bible for themselves; but alas, they cannot in countries like Saudi -Arabia where the Bible is a forbidden book!

However, consider also this possibility, muslims: If Islam is nót the true religion, and if Allah is nót the true God, than it is understandable that Allah would not want you to read this book, and cause Islamic opposition against true Christian books! Why else are Allah and you so afraid of the Bible and true Christian books? Can you explain that? Anyone who lives in deception does not know he is in deception unless he is able to look over the wall of his prison of deception. It is obvious that the deceiver does not want that! Because it would mean that his deception would be exposed. And the deceived who did not know they were deceived, would know! So, muslims, all I am inviting you to do, is for you to look over the wall. If you are not deceived, looking over

VIII

the wall will not make you deceived; it would only make you happy that you are not deceived and that those outside your wall of Islam are, and you would know better how to help them. But if, on the other hand, you wóuld find out that you are deceived in Islam, would you not want to know that? So, either way, you are better of by reading the Bible, and true Christian books.

The fear of the Bible and of true Christian books, is significantly suspicious of the one who wants to keep you in bondage to his deception! Though in no place in the Koran does Allah forbid muslims to read the Bible or Christian books. Allah says that the Koran is "the truth from your lord." How will muslims know this is true, unless they check it out? If it is true that the Koran is the truth, muslims will only be strengthened by checking it out. But if the Koran is nót the truth, muslims should find out. And if Allah does not want muslims to check it out, it raises my suspicions about who Allah really is. Because only dictators and deceivers do not want their people to know what is on the other side of the fence; therefore they allow only one message to be heard; they control the media, etc. But in Islam another very effective deception is the accusation that Christians and Jews have tampered with the Scriptures, so muslims are kept from reading and considering the Scriptures. Muslims seem so afraid of Allah, that the fact that Allah said it is enough for them. Especially since Allah intimidates them that if they question what he said, they are in danger of blasphemy, even when their questions come from an honest inquiring heart and mind. That Saudi-Arabia has forbidden the Bible, Christian literature and all Christian gatherings, as well as other expressions of Christianity in true freedom, is significant. It raises my suspicions! Why are they so afraid? Because muslims will find out the truth about Islam and abandon it? Why else forbid it?

God, on the other hand, is not afraid of anything or anyone! God invites and challenges people to really do research, and investigate His Word, and everything around us, in all freedom without any restrictions! He knows that true research, and true investigation will only lead us to Him in greater appreciation, worship, glorification and honour of Him. Not from a rite, like muslims do, but from our heart! It is significant that true science originated within Christianity. True science will always lead toward God, not away from Him (those are pseudo-sciences like 'evolution', 'psychiatry,' 'psychology,' etc.!) True science will always confirm the Word of God, the Bible! True science will always glorify God! Because of our questioning in Christianity, countless inventions have been made which enormously benefited mankind.

Allah wants muslims to simply accept the status quo of 7-th century Islam. Because there is no progress resulting from questioning in Islam, it is absolutely static. The rites performed by muslims are the same as those by muslims 1300 years ago. God, on the other hand is a Father, Who loves to hear His children ask Him many questions. Children learn by asking their parents many questions, and they do! And good parents love to answer their children! Children grow in knowledge this way. But Allah, who does not want to be a father, if questioned, is stern and angry. He may turn against the person asking him questions and accuse him of unbelief. Muslims are required by Allah to accept what Allah said without question. But how can they grow if this is so? They will remain like programmed robots, programmed with 7-th century Islamic confessions and rites, until they die, in the same state of mind all of their lives. If this is so, why serve a god like Allah? Out of fear? Muslims, look around you. What can Allah do to you in this life? Nothing! Except by other muslims! But by himself? Have you ever heard of Allah doing anything against any muslim who investigated the Koran and Islam? And since you have no way of telling if Allah is going to allow you in Islamic Paradise or not, you might as well find out if your religion and the Koran are true. If you find out the truth, Allah can only reward you for it! And if you find out that the Koran and Islam are not true, then you are also the better of, because you will be delivered from the fear of Allah which kept you so afraid and in such bondage to Allah's laws.

To Christians this book not only reveals much about Islam and the spirit behind it; it also reveals much about Christ and Christianity and thus strengthens your faith!

* Note 1: D. v.d. Meulen was born in Laren, Netherlands, on 4 September 1894. In 1923, after having worked for 8 years for the Interior Government in the Dutch-Indies, he was appointed as the successor of the Dutch Consul in Djeddah in Saudi-Arabia. After a short interruption he was again ordered to the post in Djeddah in 1941. After World War II he was sent to Batavia, Dutch-Indies, as advisor of

X

dr. van Mook. He returned to the Netherlands in 1948, where he was ordered to set up the Arabic Department of Radio Netherlands World Service. He retired in 1952, after which he made still many more information-trips to the new Arabia. He wrote 4 books in Dutch and 4 in English.

Note 2: In quotes of the Koran, "D" means the quote is taken from the Koran-version by Dawood, and "A" the version by Arberry.

Chapter One

Allah has no son

A very simple answer to the question "Are Allah and God one and the same?", comes from the fact that Islam shouts from the housetops that Allah has no son. This is one of the basic confessions of Islam, (as one of the basic confessions of communism is "Boga njet," or translated "There is no God.")

If one knows the history of the development of Islam one would know that by this confessed belief Mohammed resisted the Christian view that God has a Son, by the Name of Jesus Christ. Islam's denial that Allah has a Son, as is stated numerous times in the Koran, already qualifies Islam as a fundamentally anti-christian religion! For the Word of God, the Bible, says, "*Who is the liar but he who denies that Jesus is the Christ? He is anti-christ who denies the Father and the Son. Whoever denies the Son does not have the Father either; he who acknowledges the Son has the Father also.*" (1 John 2:22,23)

The Koran says: "*Say: 'Allah is one, the-eternal-god. He begot none, nor was he begotten. None is equal to him.'*" (The whole Sura 112) According to the Koran, Jesus, as a baby in his cradle, said: "*I am the servant of Allah. He has given me the book and ordained me a prophet.*" (Muslims reject the Gospels written by Matthew, Mark, Luke and John, as not being the Injil, the Gospel, this book that Jesus in this Sura said Allah had given him. But the Koran does not explain how this book came with Jesus. Was Jesus born with this book? Muslims believe that the Koran confirms this Injil, this book, and that the four Gospels are NOT the true Injil. {Sura 5:13-15,41,48} given to Jesus. Because it is obvious, even at a glance, that the Koran does NOT confirm the four Gospels written by Matthew, Mark, Luke and John, but says many things that are clearly in conflict with them!

The Koran cannot even begin to measure up to the Gospels. The Bible says that Jesus Christ Himself is the Word of God {and even the Koran calls Jesus the word of Allah in Sura 4:171 D}. John 1:1-3, and 14 says:

1

"In the beginning was the Word, and the Word was with God, and the Word was God. He was in the beginning with God. All things were made through Him, and without Him nothing was made that was made. ... And the Word became flesh and dwelt among us, and we beheld His glory, the glory of the only begotten of the Father, full of grace and truth.")

In the Koran, Jesus in the cradle continues: "*I was blessed on the day I was born, and blessed I shall be on the day of my death; and may peace be upon me on the day I shall be raised to life.' Such was Jesus, the son of Miriam. This is the whole truth which they still doubt. Allah forbid that he himself should beget a son!*" (Sura 19:30-37 D)

In this Sura Jesus speaks of his death. Yet in Sura 4:157-160 D the Koran denies and utterly rejects that Jesus died. It says: "*They denied the truth and uttered a monstrous falsehood against Mirjam. They declared: 'We have put to death the Messiah, Jesus the son of Mirjam, the apostle of Allah.' They did not kill him, nor did they crucify him, but they thought they did (* note 2) ...they did not slay him for certain. Allah lifted him up to him.*"

"Admonish those who say that Allah has begotten a son. Surely of this they could have no knowledge, neither they nor their fathers: a monstrous blasphemy is that which they utter. They preach nothing but falsehood." (Sura 18:5 D) "

They say: 'Allah has begotten a son.' Allah forbid! Self-sufficient is he. Say: 'Those that invent falsehoods about Allah shall not prosper." (Sura 10:68 D) "

Sovereign of the heavens and the earth, who has begotten no children and has no partner in his sovereignty." (Sura 25:1 D)

"Say: 'Praise be to Allah who has never begotten a son; who has no partner in his kingdom." (Sura 17:111 D)

"Had it been his (Allah's) will to adopt a son, he would have chosen whom he pleased out of his own creation." (Sura 39:4 D)

2

"The Jews say Ezra is the son of Allah, while the Christians say the Messiah is the son of Allah. Such are their assertions, by which they imitate the infidels of old." (Sura 9:30 D)

"Have you thought on Al-Lat and Al-Uzza, and thirdly, on Manat, the other? Are you to have sons, and he (Allah) the daughters? This is indeed an unfair distinction." (Sura 53: 20 D)

The last line of Sura 53:20 replaced the earlier **"satanic verses"** as they were later labelled, of which Allah in Sura 22:51 assures Mohammed that all the prophets and apostles before him had the same thing happen to them of satan interjecting verses according to their wishes.

It says:
"Never have we sent a single prophet or apostle before you with whose wishes satan did not tamper. But Allah abrogates the interjections of satan and confirms his own revelations.... He (Allah) makes satan's interjections a temptation for those whose hearts are diseased (Note *) *or hardened- this is why the wrongdoers are in open schism - so that those who are endowed with knowledge may realize that this* (the Koran) *is the truth from your lord."*

Allah, admits in this Sura the fact that Mohammed because of his own wishes for certain verses from Allah, like the wish Mohammed had for Allah to approve his marriage with the wife of his adopted son; which Allah, sure enough gave, according to Mohammed's desire, received verses of satan, declared these verses of Allah. Allah says in this Sura to have these "satanic verses" abrogated and replaced with new verses. But the statement that the prophets and apostles who wrote the Bible, had the same happen to them, is absolutely and totally untrue. However it was the solution Mohammed found to the problem that he was accused by his followers to be like the infidels because these verses, later ascribed to satan, acknowledged more gods.

These verses, according to Allah, afterward were 'interjected by satan because of the wish' of Mohammed to be accepted by the Meccans. In the pressing situation in Mecca Mohammed had sought acceptance by the Meccans by reciting these verses. They had immediately accepted him because these verses acknowledged their other gods. However, Mohammed, by the comments of his own followers, quickly came to realize that this totally jeopardized his whole movement and all he had set out to do. Therefore these 'satanic verses' had to be replaced, if he was to go on as messenger of Allah.

The reason for bringing the attention to the daughters of Allah, named Al-Lat, Al-Uzza, and Manat, is that they form the explanation to Mohammed's rejection that God has begotten a Son. For in the idolatry of Arabia Allah had daughters ascribed to him, and Mohammed rejected polytheism. The idea of God having begotten a Son, therefore brought a vehement reaction to Mohammed, because that would mean a return to ancient Arabian idolatry. And this is mentioned as such in the Koran.

In the verse just quoted last Mohammed also hints to the idea that daughters are inferior to sons, and how could Allah get the inferior and people the superior? That would be unfair. So, the background of Mohammed, his rejection of polytheism, and his preaching of monotheism, were the very reason that he also rejected that God had begotten a Son.

Yet in the Koran Mohammed does speak of Jesus being born of a virgin, without a man having touched her. (Sura 19:20 D)
There are many more verses in the Koran repeating that Allah has not begotten a son.

*Note: an often seen expression in the Koran: "in whose hearts is sickness", meaning those opposing Mohammed. Example: Sura 2:10.
* Note 2: Or, literally, 'he was made to resemble another for them.'

Chapter Two

Jesus Christ is God

The Koran also rejects that Jesus Christ is God. It says:
"Then Allah will say: 'Jesus, son of Miriam, did you ever say to mankind: 'Worship me and my mother as gods beside Allah? ' " (Sura 5:116 D) Muslims believe that the doctrine of the Trinity teaches God to be Three, namely the Father, Mary and Jesus. Christians may laugh at this absurd idea, but Pagans all over the world worshipped a mother and child long before the Roman Catholic and Orthodox churches incorporated it in their doctrines, even calling Mary: "Mother of God." This blasphemy of the Roman Catholic and Orthodox churches is rejected by the Bible and all Bible-believing Christians!

"People of the Book (Christians)*, do not transgress the bounds of your religion. Speak nothing but the truth about Allah. The Messiah, Jesus the son of Miriam, was no more than Allah's apostle and his word which he cast to Miriam: a spirit from him. So believe in Allah and his apostles and do not say: 'Three."* (against the Trinity) *Allah is but one god. Allah forbid that he should have a son"*(Sura 4:171 D)

"The Messiah, the son of Miriam, was no more than an apostle: other apostles passed away before him. His mother was a saintly woman. They both ate earthly food." (Sura 5:75 D)

Worse yet, the Koran calls the Christians unbelievers: *"Unbelievers are those who declare: 'Allah is the Messiah, the son of Miriam.'" "Unbelievers are those that say: 'Allah is the Messiah, the son of Miriam.'" "Unbelievers are those that say: 'Allah is one of three.'"* (Sura 5:17, 72, 73 D)

Having branded Christians as 'unbelievers' the Koran says *"The unbelievers are your inveterate enemies."* (Sura 4:101 D)

"Seek out your enemies relentlessly." (Sura 4:104 D)

"They are unbelievers who say, 'Allah is the Third of Three.' No god is there but one Allah. If they refrain not from what they say, there shall afflict those of them that disbelieve a painful chastisement. " (Sura 5:73 A)

"Proclaim a woeful punishment to the unbelievers, except to those idolaters who have honoured their treaties with you in every detail and aided none against you. With these keep faith, until their treaties have run their term. Allah loves the righteous. When the sacred months are over slay the idolaters (those with whom the treaties were made) *wherever you find them. Arrest them, besiege them, and lie in ambush everywhere for them."* (Sura 9:4,5 D) This verse is claimed to have cancelled no less than 124 verses that call for tolerance, forbearance and patience.

"This is the recompense of those who fight against Allah and his messenger, and hasten about the earth, to do corruption there: they shall be slaughtered, or crucified, or their hands and feet shall alternately be struck off, or they shall be banished from the land." (Sura 5:37 A)

From the Jews a next verse says, " *They hasten about the earth, to do corruption there*" (verse 69 A)

In the Koran Allah calls the Jewish religious leaders "*satans*," "*devils.*" (Sura 2; 13 A, Sura 2: 15 D)

"They are unbelievers who say, 'Allah is the Messiah, Miriam's son.' "

"Fight (physically!) *against such of those to whom the Scriptures were given as believe neither in Allah nor in the last day, who do not forbid what Allah and his apostle* (Mohammed) *have forbidden, and do not embrace the true faith* (Islam), *until they pay tribute out of hand and are utterly subdued.* " (Sura 9:29 D) This verse is quoted by islamic theologians to support their continual war against Israël.

Besides that, the minority groups of Jews and Christians in islamic countries have from the beginning had to pay far more taxes than muslims, so called to pay for their protection as they were not allowed to bear arms, and be part of the armed forces, as muslims feared they would use these against them.

That Jesus Christ is God is already evidenced by John 1:1-3,14 that I quoted earlier. I deal with this subject exclusively in one chapter of my complete treatise "*A Christian Defence Against Accusations of Islam.*"

Here I just want to say that **Jesus Christ is the only begotten Son of God**. Unlike Christians, who have become a child of God by spiritual birth in Christ Jesus (John 1:12,13; Galatians 3:26-29) **Jesus Christ is not á son of God, but thé Son of God**. The Jews in their culture understood this expression right away as an expression that signifies Jesus Christ to be equal with God. (For which they accused Jesus Christ of blasphemy. And it was for this very reason that they had Jesus Christ put to death.) Unlike Christians who have become children of God by their faith in Jesus Christ, Jesus Christ was begotten of God. Jesus Christ was and is the **only** begotten of God. Human beings (apart from Adam and Eve) all have a human father and a human mother. Jesus Christ did not have a human father. His Father is God! Jesus is divine seed! He was born without inherited sin. (Exodus 20:5) In this He is unique in all history!

Can therefore Allah and God ever be the same? The answer is already clear now. For God has begotten a Son, while Allah has not begotten anyone!

The true archangel Gabriel, sent out by God as His messenger to announce to virgin Mary that she was to conceive a son, by the Holy Spirit, said,
"*Do not be afraid, Mary, for you have found favour with God. And behold, you will conceive in your womb and bring forth a Son, and shall call His name JESUS. He will be great, and will be called the Son of the Highest; and the Lord God will give Him the throne of His father David. And He will reign over the house of Jacob forever, and of His kingdom there will be no end. Then Mary said to the angel, "How can this be, since I do not know a man (that is, am a virgin)? And the*

angel answered and said to her, "The Holy Spirit will come upon you, and the power of the Highest will overshadow you; therefore, also, that Holy One who is to be born will be called the Son of God." (Luke 1:30-36)

Because of the accusation of the Koran that Christians believe in three gods, and because the Muslim mind by now may have already concluded that I also make mention of three Gods, namely the Father, the Son and the Holy Spirit, I need to briefly address the issue.

The Scripture quoted above says that Mary got pregnant of Jesus Christ by the Holy Spirit. And Matthew 1:18 b states: *"She (Mary) was found with child of the Holy Spirit;"* the NBG Dutch version says, translated: *"She was pregnant of the Holy Spirit."* And Matthew 1:20b says: *"That which is conceived in her is of the Holy Spirit"*. The Scriptures therefore clearly repeatedly state the Holy Spirit to be the Father of Jesus Christ.

But the Scriptures also say that Jesus Christ is the only begotten Son of the Father (John 1:14), and that Jesus Christ is the only begotten Son of God (John 3:16) And that Jesus Christ is the Son of the Highest (Luke 1: 31,32a) So Scripture teaches that Jesus Christ, the Son of God, is begotten of the Father.

It is therefore evident that the Holy Spirit and the Father are the same One Person of God.
The Bible says: *"The Lord our God is one Lord."* (Deuteronomy 6:4) There is only one God! (Isaiah 44:8,24; Isaiah 45:18) Jesus Christ told the Father: *"I have revealed Your name"* (John 17:6) *"I have declared to them Your name."* (John 17:26 NKJV) *"I have manifested Your name* (John 17:6 NKJV) *"I have made Your name known."* (RSV, God's Word)

The name of the Father, that Jesus Christ revealed, manifested, declared and made known, is Jesus Christ! Because the Father and the Holy Spirit are the same One Person, as we have seen earlier, the name of the Holy Spirit is Jesus Christ. And the name of the Son of God is Jesus Christ. (Luke 1:31)

Clearly then the Father, the Son and the Holy Spirit are the same One Person; the same one God!

Jesus Christ told His disciples: "*the Holy Spirit, whom the Father will send in My name*." (John 14:26) The Holy Spirit therefore is in Jesus' name. Jesus also told them: "*ask the Father in My name*" (John 15: 16) The Father therefore is in Jesus' name.

Jesus told His disciples: "*And where I go you know, and the way you know.*" *Thomas said to Him, "Lord, we do not know where You are going, and how can we know the way?" Jesus said to him, "I am the way, the truth, and the life. No man comes to the Father, except through Me. If you had known Me, you would have known My Father also; and from now on you know Him and have seen Him." Philip said to Him, "Lord, show us the Father, and it is sufficient for us." Jesus said to him, "Have I been with you so long, and yet you have not known Me, Philip? He who has seen Me has seen the Father; so how can you say, 'Show us the Father'? Do you not believe that I am in the Father, and the Father in Me? The words that I speak to you I do not speak on My own authority; but the Father who dwells in Me does the works. Believe Me that I am in the Father and the Father in Me.*" (John 14:4-11 a)

John 14:26 says that the Father will send the Holy Spirit in Jesus' name, but John 15:26 says that Jesus shall send the Holy Spirit from the Father. **So, the Father and the Son are One**.

Jesus prayed: "H*oly Father, keep through Your name those whom You have given Me, that they may be one as We are. ... I do not pray for these alone, but also for those who will believe in Me through their word; that they all may be one, as You, Father, are in Me, and I in You; that they also may be one in Us, that the world may believe that You sent Me. And the glory which you gave Me I have given them, that they may be one just as We are one: I in them, and You in Me; that they may be made perfect in one , and that the world may know that You have sent Me, and have loved them as You have loved Me.*" (John 17:21 NKJV)

If all this boggles the mind of the muslim, let him not despair. It also boggles the Christian mind. All that matters here is that there is one God, and His name is Jesus Christ. Jesus Christ is the Creator (John 1:3, 10; Colossians 1:15-19). Apostle John saw One Person on the Throne of God. (Revelation 4:2)

The Bible says: "*God is Spirit.*" (John 4:24; 2 Corinthians 3: 17) Because it was necessary for a Perfect Man to die, so man could be saved and live (see the last chapter for the explanation why) as there is no remission of sins without the shedding of blood (Hebrews 9:22), God needed a body that could die, for a Spirit has no blood and cannot die. (Hebrews 2:14) Therefore God prepared Himself a body. (Hebrews 10: 5-10; Psalm 40: 6-8) Because God made man into His image (Genesis 1:27), and because God wants to co-labour and co-operate with man, since He made man, as was His plan even before the foundation of the world (Ephesians 1: 4-14), and to fulfil the prophecy of Genesis 3:15, God made Himself a body by impregnating Mary with His divine seed. (Matthew 1:18,20) *"Is there anything too hard for God?"* (Jeremiah 32:27; Luke 1:37)

The Bible says: "*God was pleased to have all of Himself live in Christ.*" (Colossians 1:19 God's Word; see also NIV, The English Bible, Amplified Version, etc.) **God did not cease to be God, when He made Himself a human body in which all of Himself lived. Though it seemed to look as if He became three Persons, He never ceased to be the same One Person of Jesus Christ: the One God, manifesting at the same time as the Father, the Son, and the Holy Spirit.**

As fully human, the Son of God prayed to God the Father. He was tempted by the devil and the world without ever giving in to sin. He was rejected. He knew feelings of utter despair, and of loneliness, and all emotions of a human being. He suffered and died at the cross of Calvary. As fully God, because the Father dwells and is in the Son (John 14 and 17) Jesus Christ still ruled the Universe, through the Spirit, omnipresent. After the Son had finished the work He came to do, He was again re-united with the Father in glory. (John 17) The muslim should know that the Christian believes in One God, not three; even when the separate manifestations of God, namely, Father, Son and holy Spirit, may confuse this.

10

Chapter Three

The way Allah is worshipped

Islam incorporated the way Allah was worshipped by Heathen Arabs.
To see this I will now go into the background of Allah. Who is Allah?

One needs to know that in Arabia before Mohammed, the different
Arab tribes had their own gods that they adored near certain shrines.
These shrines usually existed of a stone or a tree, near which the god
was understood to live. Only one single time there is mention of a
temple, like in Mecca, where the black stone, the actual object of
adoration, was built in a cubic-shaped building, called the Ka'ba. The
cult of a god belonged to a certain location. If a tribe would move from
there, it had to give up the adoration of the god of that location, and
turn to the service of the god in whose territory they had moved into.
Not only did every tribe have their own god, there also existed certain
shrines to which more tribes went up to worship a certain god. This was
the case with the god Hubal which was adored in Mecca, and to whom
a statue had been erected, though statutes of gods were rare in the
Arabic heathendom. Several tribes did also go up to adore the several
gods that had their shrines in several places around Mecca, Mina,
Muzdalifa, and Arafa. Finally there were gods that had sacred shrines
in different places in the land with different tribes. Thus several tribes,
including the people from Mecca, adored the goddesses al-Manat, al-
Lat and al-Uzza. The main shrine of the first was in Hoeidad, between
Mecca and Medina, that of the second was in Ta'if, a city east of
Mecca; and that of the third in Nachla, on the road of Ta'if to Mecca.
Apart from that there were in Mecca yet more shrines, each for other
gods.

In the time of Mohammed monotheistic tendencies had arisen. The
different people who went up to different famous shrines to exercise the
cult of the highly honoured gods everywhere encountered the same
ideas. The ceremonies that took place were practically the same. The
religious practices hardly differed from place to place. Therefore it was
easy for deeper thinkers to get the thought that it might be actually one

god that was adored in different forms and names. Next to that they increasingly met Jews and Christians which strengthened the monotheistic idea. Where earlier the god of a certain shrine had been addressed as al-Ilah or Allah, the-god, namely that of that shrine, they started to use that same name in much higher sense and 'Allah' became the name of the one that was higher than all other gods.

In a classical verse of the poet Aus ibn Hadjar from the tribe of Tamim is said, "By Allat and al-Uzza and their worshippers and by Allah and he is truely greater than they." Probably the deeper thinking Meccans considered Allah the actual owner and lord of the Ka'ba, the great shrine, to which countless numbers of worshippers made their pilgrimage. Islam incorporated this heathen pilgrimage to Mecca.

Another source says that the worldview and religion in ancient Arabia were based upon animism. Religion was of minor importance. Yet the Semites were generally quite religious, like all heathens. Even for a Semite, though he be an Arab from the tribe of the Koraish, one of the least religious tribes, it was impossible to think about political and social matters without immediately getting into religious considerations. That is why Islam does not know a separation between religion and state. As Lord Curzon remarked, *" islam is not a state-church but a church-state."* It was inevitable that the Arab would see a cause and effect connection between both.

All things that were seen, earthquakes, sounds, nightly light-effects, illnesses, etc. were not ascribed to natural causes, but to certain beings, shaped after human images, but with supernatural qualities. The most well known of these beings are the *"djinns"* .

Dozy writes in his book "Het Islamisme" (means "Islam" in Dutch) in 1863:
"The deserts and mountains, where one wanders for weeks, are full of such beings. Hunger, thirst, and the quite stimulating air of the desert, excite the spirit so much, the damps and fata morgana's are so weird, that one hears the *djinns* call; that one sees them in all kinds of weird and strange shapes. It is a generation like ours, procreating like ours, but their bodies are not like ours, they are figures of fire and light, only exceptionally visible with the human eye. They can do much harm and

much good; that is why they should be kept as friends. They dwell everywhere: in trees and plants and stones, especially those with strange and capricious shapes. One sought to use or keep out these powers, depending on the circumstances.

To communicate with the *djinns* mediators were required; these were consulted in matters of all kinds as diviners and oracles. These people, named Kahins, gave their counsel in rhymed prose, in Old Arabic, using rare and old-fashioned words. Otherwise they were not considered authentic."

It is remarkable that Mohammed recited the Koran in this fashion. *Djinns* would be considered demons by Christians, and thus many could quite easily conclude from the way of ancient poetic recitation and the circumstances in which Mohammed received his recitations, that he received them from (a) djinn (s).

Mohammed was also seen exactly as such by people of his own time. This is clearly stated in the Koran itself where we see Mohammed's defence against those who accused him of it:

"They say: 'You to whom the warning was revealed, you are surely possessed. Bring down the angels, if what you say be true.' We shall send down the angles only with the truth. Then they shall never be reprieved. It was we that revealed the Koran, and shall ourself preserve it. We have sent forth the apostles before you to the older nations: but they scoffed at each apostle we sent them. Thus do we put doubt into the hearts of the guilty: they deny him, despite the example of the ancients." (Sura 15:6 D)

"Some say:'It is but a medley of dreams.' Others: 'He has invented it himself.' And yet others:' He is a poet: let him show us some sign, as did the apostles in days gone by.' "(Sura 21:5 D)

"By the grace of Allah, you are neither a soothsayer nor a madman. Do they say:' He is but a poet...Do they say:'He has invented it (the Koran) himself'? Indeed, they have no faith. Let them produce a scripture like it, if what they say be true!" (Sura 52:29 D)

"I swear by all that you can see, and all that is hidden from your view, that this is the utterance of a noble messenger. It is no poet's speech:

scant is your faith! It is no soothsayer's divination: how little you reflect! It is a revelation of the Lord of the universe. Had he (Mohammed) *invented lies about us, we would have seized him by the right hand and severed his heart's vein: not one of you could have protected him!"* (Sura 69:42 D)

"The unbelievers say: 'This is but a forgery of his own invention, in which others (Jews and Christians) *have helped him.' Unjust is what they say and false. And they say: 'Fables of the ancients he has written: they are dictated to him morning and evening.' ...And the wrongdoers say: 'The man you follow is surely bewitched."* (Sura 25:8 D)

In several places sacred stones, or relics were found. They were adored by touching them or by smearing them with sacred ointment; they were also kissed. The most important of these was the black stone in Mecca.

Furthermore there were sacred trees; sometimes these were hanged with all kinds of pieces of garment or patches.

Then there were sacred wells, of which the well Zemzem near Mecca was one of the most important. The drinking from such a well had a special meaning.

Then there were sacred places which were adored by walking around it. These processions, seven in number, were done at a certain time, after a certain preparation. At other places one went between two points up and down.

Another practice was the pegging out of sacred area's, in which for example no blood-revenge was allowed; such an area was protected by one or more higher beings. Many of these ancient pagan Arabic practices were ended by Mohammed, others he incorporated in Islam in the ceremonies of the pilgrimage to Mecca.

Islam incorporated the following heathen way of worship of Allah:
In the center of Mecca is the Ka'ba (which means Cube), a building of 12 cubic meter, with a stone in two of the four corners, a black one and a grey one. During the procession of the Kaba the muslim pilgrims kiss these stones. The muslim pilgrims circle the Ka'ba seven times, three

times very rapidly and four times slowly. Specially prescribes 'prayers' are said. The "Place of Abraham" is visited. The muslim pilgrims drink from the sacred well, Zemzem, and run seven times between the hills of Safa and Marwa in a special way in special dress. A visit is made to Arafat, several miles from Mecca. The night is spent there and on the return journey at Mina the muslim pilgrims throw seven pebbles at the three pillars of masonry known as "First", "Middle Pillar", and "Great Devil". The ceremony is concluded on the great feast day by the offering of an animal sacrifice. After the ritual is over most muslim pilgrims visit the grave of Muhammed in Medina.

Are Allah and God the same - considering this idolatrous background of the rituals of the Islamic pilgrimage to Mecca? Rituals by which the Allah of Islam is worshipped in exactly the same way as the pagan Allah? Is it wrong to conclude that the Allah of Islam is still the ancient Arabic idol of the Ka'ba in Mecca?

God is not worshipped, honoured, or adored in a pagan way! On the contrary! God's law that He gave through His servant Moses says: *"You shall utterly destroy all the places where the nations which you shall dispossess served their gods, on the high mountains and on the hills and under every green tree. And you shall destroy their altars, break their sacred pillars, and burn their wooden images with fire; you shall cut down the carved images of their gods and destroy their names from that place. You shall not worship the Lord your God with such things."* (Deuteronomy 12:2-5 NKJV)

If God had been the same as the-god, 'Allah', all the pagan Arabic ways of worship would have been abolished and all the items involved in it would have been destroyed; the black stone in the Ka'ba, the Ka'ba, the pillars etc. would have been utterly destroyed. That is God's law!

Jesus told the Samaritan woman that the way we must worship God is in spirit and in truth. (John 4: 24) In Islam, Muslims "pray" by a multitude of recitations of the same prescribed words, in uniformed way, in public, for all to see their 'piety'.

Jesus Christ taught this about prayer: *"And when you pray, you shall not be like the hypocrites. For they love to pray standing in the synagogues and on the corners of the streets, that they may be seen by men. Assuredly, I say to you, they have their reward. But you, when you pray, go into your room, and when you have shut your door, pray to your Father who is in the secret place; and your Father who sees in secret will reward you openly. And when you pray, do not use vain repetitions as the heathen do. For they think that they will be heard for their many words. Therefore do not be like them. For your Father knows the things you have need of before you ask Him."* (Matthew 6:5-8)

And then He taught what became known as "Our Father". Christians pray from their heart, whatever they want to share with God, ask God about, request from Him, from a relationship with Him as Father.

Chapter Four

Jerusalem or Mecca

The Koran clearly says *"let them worship the lord of this house"* (the Ka'ba - Sura 106:3 D) And Mohammed says in Sura 27:91 A, *"I have only been commanded the serve the lord of this territory which he has made sacred; to him belongs everything. And I have been commanded to be of those that surrender* (Islam means surrender) *and to recite the Koran."* Therefore Allah has chosen Mecca as his city.

God on the other hand chose Jerusalem as His city, not Mecca: *"Now it came to pass, when David was dwelling in his house, that David said to Nathan the prophet, 'See now, I dwell in a house of cedar, but the ark of the covenant of the Lord is under tent curtains.' Then Nathan said to David, 'Do all that is in your heart, for God is with you.' But it happened that night that the word of God came to Nathan, saying, 'Go and tell My servant David, 'Thus says the Lord: 'You shall not build Me a house to dwell in. For I have not dwelt in a house since the time that I brought you up Israel, even to this day, but have gone from tent to tent, and from one tabernacle to another. Wherever I have moved about with all Israel, have I ever spoken a word to any of the judges of Israel, whom I commanded to shepherd My people, saying, 'Why have you not built Me a house of cedar?' Now therefore, thus shall you say to My servant David, 'Thus says the Lord of hosts: 'I took you from the sheepfold, from following the sheep, to be ruler over My people Israel. And I have been with you wherever you have gone, and have cut off all your enemies from before you, and have made you a name like the name of the great men who are on the earth. Moreover I will appoint a place for My people Israel, and will plant them, that they may dwell in a place of their own and move no more; nor shall the sons of wickedness oppress them anymore, as previously, since the time that I commanded judges to be over My people Israel. Also I will subdue all your enemies. Furthermore I tell you that the Lord will build you a house. And it shall be, when your days are fulfilled, when you must go to be with your fathers, that I will set up your seed after you, who will be of your sons; and I will establish his kingdom. He shall build Me a house, and I will establish his throne forever. I will be his Father, and*

17

he shall be My son; and I will not take My mercy away from him, as I took it from him who was before you. And I will establish him in My house and in My kingdom forever; and his throne shall be established forever.' According to all these words and according to all this vision, so Nathan spoke to David." (1 Chronicles 17:1-15 NKJV; see also 2 Samuel 7:1-17)

God through Moses had already said that He would choose a place to make His Name abide (Deuteronomy 12:11)

When Solomon had built the temple he dedicated it and said: *"Blessed be the Lord God of Israel, who has fulfilled with His hands what He spoke with His mouth to my father David,(*1) saying, 'Since the day that I brought you out of the land of Egypt, I have chosen no city from any tribe of Israel in which to build a house, that My name might be there, nor did I choose any man to be a ruler over My people Israel. Yet I have chosen Jerusalem, that My name may be there, and I have chosen David to be over My people Israel."* (2 Chronicles 6:4-6 NKJV)

"Then the Lord appeared to Solomon by night, and said to him: 'I have heard your prayer, and have chosen this place for Myself as a house of sacrifice. When I shut up heaven and there is no rain, or command the locusts to devour the land, or send pestilence among My people, if My people who are called by My name will humble themselves, and pray and seek My face, and turn from their wicked ways, then will I hear from heaven, and will forgive their sin and heal their land. Now My eyes will be open and My ears attentive to prayer made in this place. For now I have chosen and sanctified this house, that My name may be there forever; and My eyes and My heart will be there perpetually." ... *"But if you turn away and forsake My statutes and My commandments which I have set before you, and go and serve other gods, and worship them, then will I uproot them from My land which I have given them; and this house which I have sanctified for My name I will cast out of My sight, and will make it a proverb and a byword among all peoples. And as for this house, which is exalted, everyone who passes by it will be astonished and say, 'Why has the Lord done this to this land and this house?' Then they will answer, 'Because they forsook the Lord God of their fathers, who brought them out of the land of Egypt, and embraced other gods, and worshiped them and served them; therefore He has*

brought all this calamity on them." (2 Chronicles 7:12-16; 19-22 NKJV)

Israel was however quick to go after other gods; for even Solomon himself to whom the Lord had appeared twice, commanding him concerning this thing that he should not go after other gods, did not keep His commandment but bowed down to other gods. Because the foreign wives he had married - disobeying the command of God in Exodus 34:16 and Deuteronomy 7:3,4 - turned his heart after the gods that they had worshipped in their native lands, so that he did evil in the sight of the Lord (1 Kings 11:1-13). The judgment of God started with the raising up of adversaries from his midst. Then right after Solomon the kingdom was divided into two kingdoms: Israel and Juda. Israel sinned in such a way that God finally had them taken away captive to Assyria in 722 B.C. (2 Kings 17:6-23) Judah continued to live in the land until also Judah had sinned so much that God took her away captive to Babylon by the hand of Nebuchadnezzar who burned the house of God, broke down the wall of Jerusalem, burned all its palaces with fire, and destroyed all its precious possessions in 586 B.C. (2 Kings 25:8-17; 2 Chronicles 36:12-26; Jeremiah 25:8-11)

This also fulfilled the word of the Lord by the mouth of Jeremiah, until the land had enjoyed her Sabbaths to lay desolate to fulfil seventy years. *"Now in the first year of Cyrus king of Persia, that the word of the Lord by the mouth of Jeremiah might be fulfilled, the Lord stirred up the spirit of Cyrus king of Persia, so that he made a proclamation throughout all his kingdom, and also put it in writing, saying, Thus says Cyrus king of Persia: All the kingdoms of the earth the Lord God of heaven has given me. And He has commanded me to build Him a house at Jerusalem which is in Judah. Who is among you of all His people? May his God be with him, and let him go up to Jerusalem which is in Judah, and build the house of the Lord God of Israel (He is God) which is in Jerusalem. And whoever is left in any place where he dwells, let the men of his place help him with silver and gold, with goods and livestock, besides the freewill offerings for the house of God which is in Jerusalem."* (Ezra 1:1-4 NKJV)

So, a remnant of Judah and Benjamin with the priests and Levites from among them returned and rebuilt the temple in Jerusalem and its wall.

It is very remarkable that prophet Isaiah had prophesied about Cyrus about 200 years before his birth, even mentioning his exact name! A mark of a true prophet of God! (Isaiah 44:28- 45:7) (*1) This second temple and wall stood until the destruction of Jerusalem by the Romans under emperor Titus, 70 A.D., as foresaid by Jesus Christ. (Matthew 24:2,34; Mark 13:2,30; Luke 21:6,20-24) And also by the prophet Daniel (Daniel 9:25,26a). (*1) For the Jews had rejected Jesus Christ as the Son of God.

The Jews did not return to the promised land until 1948 when Israel became a nation again. There is a desire among Jews to again rebuild the temple. So far the big problem has been the fact that on the temple sight a mosque stands. But Jesus Christ said that *"Jerusalem will be trampled by Gentiles until the times of the Gentiles are fulfilled."* (Luke 21:24b) Daniel prophesied of a prince to come which shall confirm a covenant with many for one week (representing seven years) But in the middle of the week (after three and a half years) he shall bring an end to sacrifice and offering. (Daniel 9:27a) This is interpreted by many scholars that the temple will be rebuilt, and that there again will be sacrificed according to the law of Moses. The coming ruler allows them to do that for three and a half years. Then the abomination of desolation standing in the holy place (Daniel 9:27b; Matthew 24:15) and a great tribulation of three and a half years will take place *"such as has not been since the beginning of the world until this time, no, nor ever shall be. And unless those days were shortened, no flesh would be saved; but for the elect's sake those days will be shortened."* (Matthew 24:21) These three and a half years, symbolised by three and a half week in Daniel, close off the seventy weeks of which Daniel prophesied, as was told him by the mouth of the angel Gabriel: *"Seventy weeks are determined for your people and for your holy city, to finish the transgression, to make an end of sins, to make reconciliation for iniquity, to bring in everlasting righteousness, to seal up vision and prophecy, and to anoint the Most Holy."* (Daniel 9:24)

It is clear then that God has chosen Jerusalem as His city, not Mecca, nor Rome, nor Byzantium or Constantinople, nor Moscow. And God never at any time said that if Israel sinned or failed, He would choose another city instead of Jerusalem. However, from the day of Pentecost, after the resurrection and ascension of Jesus Christ, when 120 disciples of Jesus Christ, who were gathered in the Upper Room were baptised with the Holy Spirit (Acts 2:1-4), which event marked the beginning of the church, God chose to dwell in a temple not built with hands, namely the bodies of those who together make up His Body, the church. *"Do you* (Holy Spirit-filled Christians) *not know that your bodies are members of Christ? Or do you not know that your body is the temple of the Holy Spirit who is in you, whom you have from God, and you are not your own? For you were bought at a price* (the blood of Jesus); *therefore glorify God in your body and in your spirit, which are God's.* (2 Corinthians 6:15a,19,20) The first church therefore was in Jerusalem (not in Rome), and from there spread throughout the whole earth.

The church, the Bride and Body of Christ, is what God had desired and planned from even before the foundation of the world. (Ephesians 1 to 5)

Everything God did was and is towards the fulfilment of that plan. Therefore God through the mouth of His prophet Jeremiah speaks of a new covenant (Jeremiah 31:31-34). Under the first covenant God made with the Jews, God gave His written Laws. These written laws, however only required outward compliance and conformity. They could not change the person. They only made known his sin. But of the new covenant God says: *"This is the covenant that I will make with them after those days, says the Lord: I will put My laws into their hearts, and in their minds I will write them, then He adds, 'Their sins and their lawless deeds I will remember no more."* (Hebrews 10:16) *"In that He says, 'A new covenant', He has made the first obsolete. Now what is becoming obsolete and growing old is ready to vanish away."* (Hebrews 8:13) This *"new covenant is not of the letter, but of the Spirit; for the letter kills, but the Spirit gives life."* (2 Corinthians 3:6)

As the first covenant was dedicated by Moses with the blood of calves and goats, the new covenant was dedicated by Jesus Christ with His own blood. (Hebrews 9:11-28) Spirit-filled Christians are now God's living temples that he dwells in by His Spirit. From the beginning of the church God is building Himself a spiritual house with living stones: *"Coming to Him* (Jesus Christ)*as to a living stone, rejected indeed by*

21

men (His own who crucified Him), *but chosen by God and precious, you also, as living stones, are being built up a spiritual house, a holy priesthood, to offer up spiritual sacrifices acceptable to God through Jesus Christ. Therefore it is also contained in the Scripture, 'Behold, I lay in Zion* (not in Mecca; and it is not a concrete stone; stone is used here symbolically!) *a chief cornerstone* (Jesus Christ), *elect, precious, and he who believes on Him will by no means be put to shame.' Therefore, to you who believe, He is precious; but to those who are disobedient, 'The stone which the builders rejected has become the chief cornerstone,' and 'A stone of stumbling and a rock of offence.' They stumble, being disobedient to the word, to which they also were appointed. But you* (the Christians) *are a chosen generation, a royal priesthood, a holy nation. His own special people, that you may proclaim the praises of Him who called you out of darkness into His marvelous light; who once were not a people but are now the people of God, who had not obtained mercy but now have obtained mercy."* (1 Peter 2:4-10 NKJV)

The unbelieving but religious Jews, who reject the new covenant dedicated with the blood of Jesus Christ, are the ones who will rebuild the temple and sacrifice according to the old covenant.

Even after the destruction of Jerusalem by the Romans God did not choose for Himself another city. God did not choose Mecca. He did not choose Rome, nor Byzantium, nor Moscow, nor any other city. But He showed the Apostle John He Himself is building a new Jerusalem: *"Now I saw a new heaven and a new earth, for the first heaven and the first earth had passed away. Also there was no more sea. Then I, John, saw the holy city, New Jerusalem, coming down out of heaven from God, prepared as a bride adorned for her husband. And I heard a loud voice from heaven saying, 'Behold, the tabernacle of God is with men, and He will dwell with them, and they shall be His people, God Himself will be with them and be their God. And God will wipe away every tear from their eyes; there shall be no more death, nor sorrow, nor crying. There shall be no more pain, for the former things have passed away.' Then He who sat on the throne said, 'Behold, I make all things new.' And He said to me, 'Write, for these words are true and faithful.' And He said to me, 'It is done! I am the Alpha and the Omega, the Beginning and the End. I will give of the fountain of the water of life freely to him who thirsts. He who overcomes shall inherit all things, and I will be his God and he shall be My son. But the cowardly, unbelieving, abominable, murderers, sexually immoral, sorcerers, idolaters, and all liars shall have their part in the lake which burns with fire and brimstone, which is the second death.'"*

Then he writes down the description of New Jerusalem he saw, a fantastic city like a cube, 1400 miles (2253 km) long, wide and high, with a wall 200 feet (60,96 m) thick! The wall is of jasper, the city of pure gold, like clear glass; its streets of pure gold, like transparent glass. Its twelve foundations of respectively jasper, sapphire, chalcedony, emerald, sardonyx, sardius, chrysolite, beryl, topaz, chrysoprase, jacinth, amethyst. Its twelve gates are twelve pearls; each individual gate is of one pearl. *"But I saw no temple in it, for the Lord God Almighty and the Lamb are its temple. The city had no need of the sun or of the moon to shine in it, for the glory of God illuminated it. The Lamb is its light. And the nations of those who are saved shall walk in its light, and the kings of the earth bring their glory and honour into it. Its gates shall not be shut at all by day (there shall be no night there). And they shall bring the glory and the honour of the nations into it. But there shall by no means enter it anything that defiles, or causes an abomination or a lie, but only those who are written in the Lamb's Book of Life. And he showed me a pure river of water of life, clear as crystal, proceeding from the throne of God and of the Lamb. In the middle of its street, and on either side of the river, was the tree of life, which bore twelve fruits, each tree yielding its fruit every month. The leaves of the tree were for the healing of the nations. And there shall be no more curse, but the throne of God and of the Lamb shall be in it, and His servants shall serve Him. They shall see His face, and His name shall be on their foreheads. There shall be no night there: They need no lamp nor light of the sun, for the Lord God gives them light. And they shall reign for ever and ever. Then he said to me, 'These words are faithful and true.' And the Lord God of the holy prophets sent His angel to show His servants the things which must shortly take place. 'Behold, I am coming quickly! Blessed is he who keeps the words of the prophecy of this book.' Now I, John, saw and heard these things. And when I heard and saw, I fell down to worship before the feet of the angel who showed me these things. Then he said to me, 'See that you do not do that. For I am your fellow servant, and of your brethren the*

*prophets, and of those who keep the words of this book. Worship God.'
And he said to me, 'Do not seal the words of the prophecy of this book,
for the time is at hand. He who is unjust, let him be unjust still; he who
is filthy, let him be filthy still; he who is righteous, let him be righteous
still; he who is holy, let him be holy still.' 'And behold, I am coming
quickly, and My reward is with Me, to give to every one according to
his work. I am the Alpha and the Omega, the Beginning and the End,
the First and the Last.' Blessed are those who do His commandments,
that they may have the right to the tree of life, and may enter through
the gates into the city. But outside are dogs and sorcerers and sexually
immoral and murderers and idolaters, and whoever loves and practices
a lie. 'I, Jesus, have sent My angel to testify to you these things in the
churches. I am the Root and the Offspring of David, the Bright and
Morning Star.'"* (Revelation 21:1-8; 22-22:16 NKJV) So the new city
of God is not even the old Jerusalem, but the New Jerusalem, now
being built by God Himself!

* 1: Note: **God fulfills His Word!**

Chapter Five

God fulfils His Word, the Bible

That God must be the author of the Bible is also clear from the prophecies He spoke as recorded in the Bible, and from their fulfilment in minute detail.

The book *"Evidence that Demands a Verdict, Volume 1"* by Josh McDowell (Campus Crusade for Christ 1972) lists 61 Messianic prophecies which Jesus Christ fulfilled, with their references in the Old Testament where they were prophesied concerning the Messiah to come, and the references in the New Testament with the account of their fulfilment in Jesus Christ. Many of these prophecies were absolutely beyond any human control. For example, Jesus' place of birth. (Micah 5:2). His time of birth. (Daniel 9:25; Genesis 49:10) His manner of birth. (Isaiah 7:14) The exact payment of 30 pieces of silver prophesied to be paid to the traitor for betraying Jesus. Then the buying of the Potter's Field after the traitor, Judas, in his remorse had thrown the money back to the religious leaders who had paid him. (Zechariah 11:13b) In this prophecy in in Zecharaiah alone we find in the prophecy and the fulfilment the following: 1. Betrayed 2. By a friend 3. for 30 pieces (not 29, or 31 or whatever) 4. Of silver (not of gold) 5. Thrown down (not placed) 6. In the House of the Lord (no other place) 7. They bough the Potter's Field with the money as prophesied, not something else. For a human this all is amazing and impossible. But for God it's not! Other prophecies that were beyond human control were those in which is prophesied how the people would react by mocking Him, spitting Him, staring at him, etc., and also the prophecies concerning Jesus Christ's burial.

Peter Stoner in *Science Speaks* (Moody Press, 1963) writes that by using the modern science of probability "we find that the chance that any man might have lived down to the present time and fulfilled all the 8 Messianic prophecies he listed, is 1 in 10 to the 17-th power! To help us understand this staggering probability Stoner illustrates it by supposing that "we take 10 to the 17-th power silver dollars and lay them all over the state of Texas. They will cover all of the state two feet deep. Now mark one of these silver dollars and stir the whole mass thoroughly all over the state. Then blindfold a man and tell him that he can travel wherever he wished in Texas, but he must pick out that one marked silver dollar without looking. The chance for him to find that marked silver dollar is the same as for the prophets to write these 8 prophecies and have these all come true in one man, from the day the prophecies were prophesied to the present time, provided they wrote these prophecies from their own mind. Now these prophecies were either given by inspiration of God or the prophets just wrote them as they thought they should be. In such a case the prophets had just one chance in 10 to the 17-th power of having these 8 prophecies come true in any man, but they all came true in Christ. This means that the fulfilment of these 8 prophecies alone proves that God inspired the writing of those prophecies to a definiteness of only one chance in 10 to the 17-th power of being absolute. Stoner considers 48 Messianic prophecies and says, "we find the chance that any one man fulfilled all 48 prophecies to be 1 in 10 to the 157-th power! And Jesus Christ fulfilled not just 48 prophecies, but 332 prophecies in the Old Testament, prophesied over a 1500 year time period! So, the Bible can only clearly have been from the mind of God, as no human could ever come up with such a thing.

Peter Stoner also calculated the probability that the prophecies God gave concerning the city of Tyre, Samaria, Gaza and Ashkelon, Jericho, The Golden Gate, Zion Plowed, Jerusalem enlarged, Palestine, Moab and Ammon, Edom, and Babylon, could have been fulfilled by chance, if they had been originated in the human mind, a chance of 1 in 5,76 times 10 to the 59-th power. So, again the possibility is excluded that a human being could have ever written those prophecies from his human mind! Yet, these prophecies have all been fulfilled in detail! Tyre: Ezekiel 26:3-21; Sidon, Tyre's sister city: Ezekiel 28:22,23, Samaria: Hosea 13; Micah 1:6, Gaza-Ashkelon: Amos 1:8; Jeremiah 47:5; Zephaniah 2:4-7, Moab-Ammon: Ezekiel 25:3,4; Jeremiah 48:47; Jeremiah 49:6, Petra and Edom: Isaiah 34:6-15; Jeremiah 49:17,18; Ezekiel 25:13,14; Ezekiel 35:5-7, Thebes and Memphis (Egypt): Ezekiel 30:13-15, Nineveh: Nahum 1:8,10; 2:6; 3:10,13,19, Babylon:

Isaiah 13: 19-22; Isaiah 14: 23; Jeremiah 51: 26,43, Jerusalem's enlargement: Jeremiah 31: 38-40, Palestine: Leviticus 26: 31-33; Ezekiel 36: 33-35. These prophecies have all been quoted, and the account of their fulfilment in history have all been listed, in chapter 11 of "Evidence that Demands a Verdict," by Josh McDowell.

We see none of this in the Koran. The Koran cannot even compare to the Bible!

Chapter Six

The name Allah

Deception by a wrong translation

The aim of this chapter is to show that the translation of Allah as God, and of God as Allah, is a grammatical error, and that because of the wrong translation many are deceived and conclude that Allah and God are one and the same.

Furthermore, Allah is dressed up with names that do NOT suit him, because his true character as revealed in the Koran, is very different than the names given him. The fact that Mohammed dressed the ancient Arabic idol Allah with attributes etc. of God that he had borrowed from Bible-stories and doctrines of Christian sects that he was told, does not change the nature of Allah. Here again people are deceived by names Mohammed thus cloaked Allah with, to think that since these names are similar to attributes of God, that Allah and God must be the same. The following illustration may help to understand: A look alike of queen Elizabeth of England may dress up like her and learn to act and talk like her, but she is quickly unmasked by those who truly know her. But those who don't know her, especially if they are far from her in place and/or time, may easily be fooled by the look alike who may even take upon herself the authority of queen Elizabeth.

It is clear by the dialogue that 'Christians' of the Roman- Catholic Church, the Reformed Church, churches of the Council of Churches, participate in with muslims – a dialogue that requires that both parties respect the other party as of equal value, which muslims can not do (as they fully well know, but they are allowed to feign their respect, when in fact their aim for initiating the dialogue is to gain respect and in the end to take over!) and which true Christian can not do, as this is a denial of Jesus Christ! – do nót know God at all. Those who do NOT know God, are easily fooled by the false dress Mohammed put on the idol of Mecca, Allah, to think he may be God. Those who know God are not so easily fooled! Every time that muslims initiate a dialogue with 'christians,' they require them to agree with their condition: "We worship the same God." Which is: the muslims want Christians to enter into this lie, and by doing this, to make a contract with satan, the 'father of lies.'(John 8)

Even though Mohammed in his middle Mecca period also quite frequently used the name 'ar-Rahman', which means 'the merciful One', this does not make Allah equal with the true Merciful One: God of the Bible. It is unsure where Mohammed derived that name from. Earlier it was thought to be derived from Syrian Christians who indeed did know this expression. Later, however, more and more South-Arabic inscriptions were found after which it was more and more attributed to be South-Arabic. For among these inscriptions there are several from monotheistic circles, where **God** is addressed as **Ilah**, as well as with ar-Rahman. After this middle Mecca period Mohammed used the address ar-Rahman no more, for fear of being accused of addressing two gods, though he declared with force that they were one and the same, "*Say:'It is the same whether you call on Allah or on the Merciful: His are the most gracious names.' "* (Sura 17:110) Christian texts from Southern Arabia speak of ar-Rahman and his Messiah and the Holy Spirit, or of ar-Rahman and His Son, Christos, the victorious One.

Early South-Arabian Christians, as well as other monotheistic circles, therefore **used to address God with Ilah**, not with Allah.

The word '*allah*' is a contraction of '*al-ilah*,' which translated means: '*the-god.* ' The word 'man' is a neutral undefined word. But when the name of a person replaces the word 'man', the word becomes defined by the man with that name. If someone calls "man" many may respond. If they call out a name, only the person by that name responds, especially when some characteristics of the addressed person are added to it. The same it is with God. There is in truth only one God, and the rest are idols though addressed as 'god' by their followers. The word 'god' is a neutral word, just as the word man, woman, etc.

In the West idols are addressed as 'god' with a small 'g', while God of the Bible is addressed as 'God' with a capital 'G.' The use of the capital

'G' therefore already defines and determines God of the Bible. The word 'God' with a capital 'G' therefore is no longer a neutral undefined word. But God did reveal His name, because in speech there is no difference between a small 'g' and a capital 'G.' So, to make sure we address God, we address Him by the name He revealed.

Idol-worshippers address the-god they want to get in touch with by using it's name. A name given to the title brother, sister, man, woman, god, etc. determines the title and is therefore no longer undefined but addresses the person or god by that name. Yehovah is the Name of God, by which only One is addressed.

'Ila'h is the unspecified, neutral Arabic word which means 'god.' Any god may respond to that address, and there are many, behind which are demons.

That is why it was so marvelous that God first revealed His name to Moses. Later Jesus Christ revealed, declared and made known the Name of God (John 17: 6 and 26) by which He was to be addressed from then on. He said: "Most assuredly, I say to you, whatever you ask the Father in My name He will give you. Until now you have asked nothing in My name. Ask, and you will receive that your joy may be full." (John 16: 23b,24) No one else but God can be addressed by the use of His Name.

If someone writes out a check to me and I want to cash it, if he has an account and enough in the bank, I can cash the check. But if he is not known there, it's a worthless peace of paper. Thus it matters greatly what name is behind it, which means, what person is behind the name. For a person and his name are inseparable. If I send out a letter I better put the right name and address on it if it is to reach the one I want to reach. Oh, there is much depth in this!

Jesus has validated checks to the heavenly bank, so to speak, that we can exchange because He has already signed them with His name. Our receiving from God also proves that Jesus Christ is alive and that He is God! His actions according to His Word prove His Word to be the Word of God! He backs up His Word with His actions, to this very day! A whole study can be made about the depth and practical use of "In

Jesus' Name." Since Jesus Christ's resurrection from the dead and ascension into the heavens no checks can be cashed in the heavenly bank that do not bear the name of Jesus Christ, and do not have Jesus Christ's signature on them.

So it is a great abomination that in Arabic, and in other languages of predominantly islamic nations, always Allah is addressed, even by Christians who, in fact, want to refer to Yehovah. Because in Arabic and these languages the undefined word for god, 'ilah', has been replaced by the defined word 'Allah,' which definition is like a name. In 'Allah' the article 'al' (meaning 'the') prefixes the title-word 'ilah.' As I pointed out earlier, the word '*Allah*' is a contraction of 'al' and 'ilah' and therefore means 'the-god,' NOT 'god' or 'God.' **The word '*Allah*' is therefore no longer neutral and undefined** (like 'god,' man, woman, etc.), **but defined, like a name, pointing to 'the-god' of Mecca, the ancient Arabic idol.**

The resulting confusion has even corrupted many so called Christian missionaries, who may have came too close to clearly see and discern that Allah of Islam is NOT God of the Bible, but the same being that was behind the ancient idol in Mecca. Many of them may have allowed their desire for a common ground to reach the muslims, to clutter their view and spiritual understanding. Others are simply tainted by the spirit of Islam.

Is it a wonder that islamic society is so dark and oppressive? That darkness is now allowed entrance into our societies by humanistic authorities and humanistic so called Christians, who are pursuing a dialogue with Islam. A pseudo-peace with muslims at the expense of the truth! As a dialogue pre-supposes respect for the views of each of the both sides, the pseudo- christians by doing so, deny the truth: they deny Jesus Christ! Muslims may show outward signs of respect, but they cannot, without denying Islam, have respect for Christianity either. But Islam allows muslims to do as if they respect Christianity, as long as the true intention in their heart is their pursuit of the furtherance of Islam by it! Oh, how naive, blinded, gullible and arrogant are those pseudo-christians! How they serve the devil well! They certainly do not serve the muslims themselves, because by their dialogue with muslims, they do not bring the muslims to a saving knowledge of Jesus Christ, and disobey the command of the Lord Jesus Christ to also make them His disciples! The dialogue keeps the muslims in their darkness and in their un-regenerated state: lost for eternity! The humanistic kind of pseudo-love these pseudo-christians are motivated by to have the dialogue, is the kind of love that does not warn people for their upcoming doom and letting them perish, even aiding them in it! It is not love at all; it is the kind of deception and hatred that is found in satan. And this therefore reveals the spirit behind the dialogue: satan!

Do I write all this to hurt Muslims? No, not at all. *Jesus said to those who believed in Him, "If ye continue in my word, then are ye my disciples indeed; And ye shall know the truth, and the truth shall make you free." ..."If the Son therefore shall make you free, ye shall be free indeed." (John 8:31,32,36)* Therefore I want all people to know the truth or at least to be given an opportunity to make a choice for the truth. But how can they believe in the truth, how can they choose for the truth, how can they know the truth and thereby be made free when the truth is not allowed to speak out and make itself heard, either by allowing the dictatorship of Islam to limit the freedom of it's expression in the press even in the West by the accusation of "the truth being an insult to Muslims", or by explicit exercise of that totalitarian dictatorship in countries of Islam, Hinduïsm, or whatever predominant religion or ideology that fears to loose control by the truth? *****Note 1.

Ilah is an undetermined title, but Allah is not. The article 'al' in 'al-ilah', contracted as 'allah', determines Allah to be 'the-god,' the idol of the Ka'ba in Mecca, whose name actually is Hubal. When Islam was decided to be the religion of Arabia, with the exclusion of all other religions, the word used in Arabic for "god" became "Allah" because in Islam no other "god" was recognised than Allah: 'the-god' of the Ka'ba of Mecca, the ancient Arabic idol, with the rejection of all other gods. Thus it became to even be accepted in the Arabic used by Christians, and even in the Bible versions in Arabic, Turkish, Bahassa Indonesia, etc.. Thus because of the language 'the-god' of Islam having monopolized the language, has now even penetrated into the Bible versions in those languages, replacing God, with Allah, 'the-god' of the Ka'ba in Mecca. This is not only factually wrong but it is also wrong grammatically, as I have explained.

The very sad thing is that because of the use of Allah in Christian texts in Arabic, and of God in translations of islamic texts, in for example the Western media, many have concluded that Allah and God are the same. Satan has really dealt a blow here. (*2) It is very serious for it is very important what name is used to address and reach the right person. Therefore Arab Christians etc. who try to address and reach God by using the name Allah are actually calling on 'the-god' of Mecca, the ancient Arab idol! Since they are not calling on God, though they intend to, they are not reaching Him because their address is wrong! Is this not a main reason why Christianity in all those languages that use the name 'Allah' instead of God, is so weak? And also a reason that so few people have been won to Christ? And of the greater danger for those few who do come to Christ to fall back?

So, also the use of the article 'al' in Allah, makes clear that Allah and God are not the same, for Allah is not Ilah. To translate Allah with God, and to translate God with Allah are therefore grammatical errors with grave consequences because of the implications. For Allah is the name of, and addresses 'the-god,' the ancient Arabic idol of the Ka'ba in Mecca. The fact that Mohammed in his twisted versions of Scripture he incorporated from stories he had heard, replaced God, Ilah, with Allah, thus replacing God with the ancient Arab idol of Mecca, does in no wise mean they are the same. Rather Allah is an impostor, even daring to dress himself with clothes, attributes, that only belong to the One God, Yehovah!, the God of the Bible! As Scripture says: "*Satan himself transforms himself into an angel of light.*" (2 Corinthians 11:14) The verse prior to that speaks of false apostles. Jesus warns His disciples for "*false prophets and false christs who will rise and show great signs and wonders to deceive, if possible even the elect.*" (Matthew 24:24) And Mohammed did not even perform one sign or wonder in all of his life!

*****Note 1: The Western governments - utterly weak by mostly jelly-fish-backboned politicians (as mice with microphones), who, for votes, are pursuing a pseudo-peace with all, even at the expense of truth, justice, morals, righteousness, etc. - refuse to deal with violant outbursts of rage by muslims, whose indignation (even when faked) is so quickly aroused, in another way than by avoiding conflict by denying the truth that the muslims so violantly respond to its expression

33

in freedom. The press in the West chooses the same pseudo-peace by avoiding conflict by censoring the truth. In this way the muslims have already succeeded in dictating the West! The price for this pseudo-peace is a stifling of the truth; the extinguishing of the light of truth, freedom, morals, virtue, etc.; the abolishing of freedoms; and increased terror and control! (The Dutch poet Bordewijk wrote: *"Als een volk voor tirannie zwicht, verliest het meer dan lijf en goed; dan dooft het licht."* Translated: **"If a people gives in to tyranny, it looses more than body and possession; than light extinguishes."**)

For Islam the thus gained territory in dictatorship is never enough until it has reached absolute totalitarian power in all nations of the world. And the West that sought to avoid conflict by accommodating for the faked 'insults' and other tactics of muslims, will find that the more Islam is accommodated, the more the muslims want to have control, and the less they are satisfied with the accommodations given! **The conflict with Islam cannot be avoided** (except by telling muslims the truth even about their own Islam, by books like this one; only if muslims embrace the truth, there is hope.); **therefore it needs to be faced with forceful and single-minded determination!**

Muslims themselves are not served with gaining territory in the Western nations. If they liked their islamic nations so much, why do they come to the West, if they hate the West so much? So if they succeed in setting up in the West the system they left, what good is that to them? And certainly it is hell for the West!

What nation wants backward 7-th century Arabic heathendom to be in control? Why is the West so naïve and so selective in their choice of information on Islam? Why does the West in general refuse to know the truth about Islam? Why does the West so gullibly swallow the deceptions, only because they love words as tolerance, dialogue, integration of other cultures (when Islam itself never accepts any other culture, religion, system etc. when in control? And Islamic control is total, absolute, totalitarian, and tolerates none other besides it!

Only when muslims are a minority do they tolerate it outwardly out of necessity, but in their hearts they hate it and always have the hidden agenda of seeking control! Wake up, West!), and hate words as

34

'discrimination' (when there is nothing wrong with that word; it simply means to distinguish. So, everybody discriminates between light and dark; wet and dry; low and high, etcetera!) and 'racism.'

All these words have been over the past decades been corrupted and polluted by ill-meaning people! Satan, whose character is clear in this language-pollution, is a deceiver, and a perverter. He perverts the truth. He perverts morals. He perverts language! He perverts everything! His only goal is the deception of mankind, and by their deception their eternal damnation! (is also *Note 2) Because of the language pollution many words have to be re-defined and explained in their original meaning before they can again be used properly! However, it is better to do that, than to give in to the language-pollution by unscrupulous figures!

Chapter Seven

The Personality of Allah is far different from the personality of God

The personality of Allah as seen in the Koran, is very different from the personality of God as seen in the Bible. Though Allah borrowed and dressed himself outwardly with attributes of God from the Bible, his true nature and character of the ancient idol of Mecca can still be determined from the Koran.

One can ask a muslim why Allah created the universe and mankind, as he is told to have done (borrowed from God). The muslim will probably answer, because it was the will of Allah. But, muslim, why was it the will of Allah? What is the purpose Allah has with his claimed creation? To exercise his will? To show himself powerful? To cast some in burning hell, and others in paradise? For what purpose? What's the use of that all? What is mankind to Allah? Did Allah only allegedly create man to have him surrender to him in Islam, as his slave? If this is all Allah wants of man, why then did Allah not create mankind as robots? If one observes muslims doing the salat, they all look like robots doing the same thing; they say the same thing, like a recording saying names of Allah and other islamic confessions, so what pleasure does this give to Allah, what purpose, what meaning does this have to Allah? May be this is not fair to ask a muslim, because he has no answer to these questions. Because Allah does not answer these questions in the Koran. But these questions have to be asked, and muslims should ask themselves these questions, for in the answers lay his way to life, to truth and to salvation.

True, most muslims will simply, like robots who do not think for themselves, answer that this is not their concern; they simply surrender and that's it; they think and act the way Allah dictates in the Koran and

Islam; that is the way they are programmed. Muslims have not learned to question these things and and are suspicious of the Western scientific and inquiring mind. For fear of the wrath of Allah, even more, for fear of the muslims around them, they do not question what they believe, confess, and practice. This is why Islam is a fatalistic religion. Everything and everyone stays the way they are. Ideal islamic society exists of people who have surrendered to be islamic robots. The Koran says Islam is the best society. (Sura 3:110) So a society of islamic robots is what the Koran considers the best society on earth. The Western mind, with it's Judeo-Christian background, however, is inquisitive, and because of this, knowledge has greatly increased, and great inventions, great improvements have been made into the human existence, of which even muslims themselves profit. Without the West, Saudi Arabia and all the oil-rich countries around them, would still be as backward and poor they ever were; not knowing they lived on such vast wealth in their soil. (I am sorry to speak in terms of 'the West', but for lack of a better term, I decided to use it because it is understood what I mean by it.)

God, on the other hand, has created the universe and all therein with a definite plan and a definite purpose. God does not do anything without a purpose. God revealed His plan and purpose in the Bible, as well as the destiny of all people! God is a logical God. Though His thoughts are higher than our thoughts and His ways higher than our ways (Isaiah 55: 8-11), He invites us to reason with Him (Isaiah 1: 16-20). Man was originally made into God's image. (Genesis 1:27) Because man was disobedient to God, this image was marred with a sinful nature that man was not originally made with by God. Through Christ man can be restored to God's original plan: man is conformed to the image of Jesus Christ (Romans 8:29; 2 Corinthians 3: 18) The reason God originally made man in His image, was that God wanted a partner, a Bride for Himself: the Church. The Bible tells us so. So God needed the men and women who are making up the Church, the Bride of Christ, to be of His nature. (more on this in the chapter in which I explain salvation). So He could communicate with them, and they with Him.

The relationship God seeks to have with men and women, is the reason for Him creating the whole universe with all it contains. To God the relationship with His Bride is His utmost priority and all is subject to it.

From this purpose God created man and woman and the whole universe for, we can understand many things from God. And from looking at man, made into the image of God, though it be in a sinfully marred state, we can still deduct and understand attributes of God; as a fingerprint identifies the individual who made this image with his finger, so man identifies the Maker of man: God.

From the relationship God wants to have with man (when I speak of man, I include woman), we can understand:

1: that God is near. God's Word says that He sticks closer than a brother. (Proverbs 18:24 b) Allah, on the other hand, is distant and cannot be reached by the muslim.

2: that God is extremely interested in the individual. He has even counted the hairs on our head. Allah is only interested in himself, and mankind is only subject to him.

3. that God is love. He loves each and every individual so much that He even gave His own Son to save him. (John 3:16 etc.) Allah knows no love. He stands on his own. He is the centre of all, apart from and high over all.

4. that God gave freedom to all. Love demanded it! Because God wants people to love Him, He had to give them freedom. Even the freedom to choose to go their own way (as most in the West now do). Love without freedom, is no love; love cannot be forced. Allah, on the other hand gives no freedom. Allah is a totalitarian dictator, where no one has any freedoms, liberties. All is strictly regulated. People are forced into islamic uniformity, forced into denying themselves in their God-given versatile personalities, qualities, creativities, harnassed according to Allah's will. The uniform way of dress of muslims is a clear example of this. God created men with an endless variety of personalities, outward appearances, etc. and thus made a multifaceted society, with a multitude of variations, colours, shapes etc.

5. that God cares. God infinitely cares for each one of us. Allah, on the other hand, does in no wise care about, nor for people, muslims

included; he only cares about himself. People are only to fulfil his own selfish desires.

6. that God is near in our suffering. Suffering is NOT the will of God, though God allows it, but never to enjoy to see us suffer; on the contrary, He suffers with us; no the only reason for Him to allow our suffering for a time is for our own good, though we may reject this idea in our human understanding. Suffering and death is NOT the will of God, nor is God to blame, but it came into the world through the disobedience of our forefather Adam; and when Adam sinned we all sinned in him (the whole human race was in Adams loins). In Islam, on the other hand, suffering is the will of Allah. The muslim can do nothing about it but to fatalistically accept it. Hospitals were therefore never a muslim idea. In the Bible God reveals the origin of death and suffering.

7. that God provided a way out. In Christ Jesus God provided the remedy for death and human suffering (and the suffering of all of creation).

Prophet Isaiah prophecies of Jesus: *"He is despised and rejected by men, a man of sorrows and acquainted with grief... He was despised, and we did not esteem Him. Surely He has borne our griefs and carried our sorrows; yet we esteemed Him stricken, smitten by God, and afflicted. But He was wounded for our transgressions, He was bruised for our iniquities; the chastisement for our peace was upon Him, and by His stripes we are healed. All we like sheep have gone astray; we have turned, every one, to his own way; and the Lord has laid on Him the iniquity of us all. He was oppressed and He was afflicted, yet He opened not Hs mouth; He was led as a lamb to the slaughter, and as a sheep before its shearers is silent, so He opened not His mouth. He was taken from prison and from judgment, and who will declare His generation? For He was cut off from the land of the living; for the transgressions of My people He was stricken. And they made His grave with the wicked- but with the rich at His death, because He had done no violance, nor was any deceit in His mouth. Yet it pleased the Lord to bruise Him; He has put Him to grief. When You make His soul an offering for sin, He shall see His seed, He shall prolong His days, and the pleasure of the Lord shall prosper in His hand. He shall see the labor of His soul, and be satisfied. By His knowledge My righteous Servant shall justify many, for He shall bear their iniquities. Therefore I will divide Him a portion with the great, and He shall divide the spoil with the strong. Because He poured out His soul unto death, and He was numbered with the transgressors, and He bore the sin of many, and made intercession for the transgressors."* (Isaiah 53:3-12 NKJV)

Allah on the other hand does not care about the suffering of the muslim; He simply willed it, and the muslim cannot ask Allah why he lets him suffer. Because Allah does it without any reason, or explanation, and does not answer such questions; neither does the Koran.

8. that God gives answers to our questions. We may ask all questions of Him we want to ask. And He promises to answer! As a Father God is interested in all of our questions, thoughts, talk; He likes to hear us talk to Him, and ask Him questions. It doesn't matter how small and insignificant it may be in our eyes; if it is important to us, it is important to God, no matter what. God always desires to spend time with us; He wants us to spend time with Him! Allah, so far and distant and unapproachable for the muslim, never answers any questions; and does not want to spend time with anyone, except with himself.

9. that God answers our prayers. God says so in His Word! Allah never promised anything to anyone in the Koran; he only demands utmost compliance with the rules, regulations and rites of Islam, from every muslim. The 'salat' (literally meaning: 'ritual prayer') is an islamic rite and ritual that has nothing to do with a prayer from the heart and mind. The muslim prostrates himself 5 times a day in the direction of Mecca while reciting names of Allah and other islamic confessions, as the playing of a recording. Because the salat is in Arabic the non-Arabic muslims, who do not speak nor understand Arabic, do not even know what they are saying in the salat! That is some 80 - 86% of all the muslims in the world!

10. that God, knowing the end from the beginning, and revealing His purposes and His destiny for His creation, especially for the people (those who accepted Jesus Christ and His accomplished work at the cross of Calvary; and those who rejected Christ Jesus' as Lord) never

40

needed to change any Word He ever spoke; what God spoke stood and stands for ever! Allah on the other hand, needed to cancel verses from the Koran and replaced them with other 'better or similar' verses. (Sura 2:106 D) Allah therefore clearly is NOT all-knowing, though Islam confesses him to be.

11. that God therefore can be trusted, and Allah cannot be trusted. One can never trust Allah, for he does what he likes, whenever he likes, with whomever he likes. God never acts against His Word. He goes by His Word. Allah does not go by his words. He does as he pleases and no can ask him why he acts against his words.

12. God gladly forgives all who turn to Him, repent and ask His forgiveness. Allah cannot be relied on; he forgives whomever he wants to forgive, and when he doesn't want to forgive, he doesn't. At the last judgment he does the same, and everybody has to fear if Allah will accept him or not. God accepts us in His Son Jesus Christ, and we can know that our sins have been forgiven and that we have eternal life in Him.

13. God guides each of His children personally by His Holy Spirit. (Romans 8: 14 - 17) Allah is far and the muslim only repeats the same rituals muslims have performed for 1300 years now. There is no life in it!

14: The Spirit of God "*helps in our weaknesses. For we do not know what we should pray for as we ought, but the Spirit Himself makes intercession for us with groanings which cannot be uttered.*" (Romans 8:26) Also Jesus Christ Himself makes intercession for us: "*Therefore He is also able to save to the uttermost those who come to Him, since He always lives to make intercession for them.*" (Hebrews 7:25) The reason for this intercession is because satan, "*the accuser of the brethren*" is bringing accusation against the saints, the true Christian, before God day and night! (Revelation 12:10) Allah, on the other hand, does none of that for the muslims.

15: Jesus Christ came to serve. "*Let this mind be in you which was also in Christ Jesus, who, being in the form of God, did not consider it robbery (something to be held onto) to be equal with God, but made*

Himself of no reputation, taking the form of a bondservant, and coming in the likeness of men. And being found in appearance as a man, He humbled Himself and became obedient to the point of death, even the death on the cross. Therefore God also has highly exalted Him and given Him the name which is above every name, that at the name of Jesus every knee should bow, of those in heaven, and of those on earth, and of those under the earth, and that every tongue should confess that Jesus Christ is Lord, to the glory of God the Father." (Philippians 2: 5-11)

Therefore Jesus Christ also wants us to have this same kind of servant-heart. *"You know that the rulers of the Gentiles lord it over them, and those who are great exercise authority over them. Yet, it shall not be so among you; but whoever desires to become great among you, let him be your servant. And whoever desires to be first among you, let him be your slave - just as the Son of Man did not come to be served, but to serve, and to give His life a ransom for many."* (Matthew 20: 25-28)

Apostle Paul also made himself a servant to all. (1 Corinthians 9:19)

Alas, power corrupts, and many 'Christian' leaders throughout history did not resist the temptation for power but succumbed to it and thereby did not obey Jesus' command nor follow His example, but instead of serving, they demanded to be served! Therefore many 'noblemen' in the Dark Ages of the 'church' became priests out of ambition for power, not to serve! Thus they have given the world a totally wrong picture of the Kingdom of God and of Christianity! Allah never came to serve. Allah serves no one but himself. To muslims the idea of Allah as a servant is weakness. In the Kingdom of God serving is a strength which brings out the best in people! No wonder hospitals and all kinds of humanitarian aid were initiated by Christians throughout history, greatly relieving the suffering of mankind!

16: God knows what it is to be human from His own human experience! He knows what it is to suffer, to be tempted, to be rejected, to be disappointed, to hurt, to be broken-hearted, etc.!

Therefore He can truelly be a High Priest! *"For it was fitting for Him, for whom are all things and by whom are all things, in bringing many*

42

sons to glory, to make the captain of their salvation perfect through sufferings. Inasmuch then as the children have partaken of flesh and blood, He Himself likewise shared in the same, that through death He might destroy him who had the power of death, that is, the devil, and release those who through fear of death were all their lifetime subject to bondage. Therefore, in all things He had to be made like His brethren, that He might be a merciful and faithful High Priest in things pertaining to God, to make propitiation for the sins of the people. For in that He Himself has suffered, being tempted, He is able to aid those who are tempted." (Hebrews 2: 10, 14, 15, 17, 18)

"For we do not have a High Priest who cannot sympathize with our weaknesses, but was in all points tempted as we are, yet without sin." (Hebrews 4:15)

"who, in the days of His flesh, when He had offered up prayers and supplications, with vehement cries and tears to Him who was able to save Him from death, and was heard because of his godly fear, though He was a Son, yet He learned obedience by the things He suffered.

Not that Jesus Christ was ever disobedient, but by experience, by His suffering, He knew what it is like to submit and obey.

And having been perfected, He became the author of eternal salvation to all who obey Him, called by God as High Priest according to the order of Melchizedek." (Hebrews 5:7-10) "consider Him who endured such hostility from sinners against Himself" (Hebrews 12: 3)

Allah, on the other hand, does not know how it feels to be human. Therefore, Allah cannot understand human experiences like suffering. Allah can therefore not be merciful, though that is one of the names he dressed himself with, stolen from God.

This is only a very brief overview of the character of God as revealed in the Bible as well as known by people's personal experiences with God, versus the character of Allah, as revealed in the Koran. And being distant, Allah is never experienced by anyone; so no one can know Allah from experience.

Muslims view the Christian idea of God being love, weak. That Allah would have love or any other emotion is unthinkable to the muslim, and considered a weakness. That Allah is harsh is acceptable to the muslim. More than any other thing the Koran impresses Allah's all-knowing, irresistable will and all-mighty power. To the muslim the view of Allah as willpower is the highest.

A Muslim questionary in which is asked "In what sense can it be said of Allah that he loves? The answer is that to Allah love is his favour towards a favoured object and that his wrath is the withholding of that favour. Here love and will are identified, for favour simply is Allah's will concerning someone. And what he wills, he fulfils by his power.

The text "God is love" does not touch the muslim, so strong any recognition of any emotional element in Allah causes the thought of some weakness or infirmity in him.

The words "the Merciful, the Compassionate" are at the beginning of every Sura in the Koran but one. What is meant by it never is a compassionate father, but the compassion of a tyrant, who for no reason at all, saves some in the general destruction.

In contrast to God, who *"is not slack concerning His promise, as some count slackness, but is longsuffering toward us, not willing that any should perish but that all should come to repentance* "(2 Peter 3:9), to Allah it does not depend on man's choice to repent resulting in his salvation from perishing, but on the will of Allah, even though there is at least one verse in the Koran that gives man a choice, like Sura 18:29 D, "*Say, this is the truth from your Lord. Let him who will, believe in it, and him who will, deny it.' For the wrongdoers We have prepared a fire which will encompass them like the walls of a pavilion. When they cry out for help they shall be showered with water as hot as molten brass, which will scald their faces.*" (Physically this is even impossible, that water can be as hot as molten brass. For long before the water would reach the temperature of molten brass, it would have become steam.)

The verses giving people a choice may well be part of those verses that have been cancelled, abrogated and replaced by the harsh intolerant, violent verses from the period of Mohammed in Medina,

for the Koran says, "*Whomsoever Allah desires to guide, he expands his breast to islam; whomsoever he desires to lead astray, he makes his breast narrow, tight*" (Sura 6:125 A) "*Whomsoever Allah guides, he is rightly guided, and whomsoever he leads astray, thou wilt not find for him a protector to direct.*" (Sura 18:17 A) "*Indeed, we sent forth among every nation a messenger, saying: 'Serve you Allah, and eschew idols.' Then some of them Allah guided, and some were justly disposed to error. So journey in the land, and behold how was the end of them that cried lies. Though thou art ever so eager to guide them, Allah guides not those whom he leads astray; they have no helpers.*" (Sura 16:39 A) "*Think! Who, besides Allah, can guide the man who makes his lust his god, the man whom Allah deliberately confounds, setting a seal upon his ears and heart and drawing a veil over his eyes?*" (Sura 45:23 D) "*Whomsoever Allah guides, he is rightly guided; and whom he leads astray- they are the losers. We have created for Gehenna many jinn and men.*" "*Whomsoever Allah leads astray, no guide he has; He leaves them in their insolence blindly wandering.*" (Sura 7:177,185 A)This is repeated in more verses. It is these verses that led to the doctrine of a predestination.

From comparing Allah as the Koran reveals him to be, and God as the Bible reveals, we can definitely conclude that they are not the same, but far different!

Except if we want to deceive ourselves and by our deliberate choice refuse to weigh the facts and evidence as presented here.

As behind all idols demons operate, behind Allah operates a definite spirit, who has control of the lives of all muslims! What darkness therefore rules in countries with a majority of islam. One cannot know that darkness as experienced in such countries from a book. I once visited Morocco, and when I entered into Ceuta, which is a part of the African continent that belongs to Spain, it was as if I had entered another world. What pressure lifted. What other atmosphere I felt. This can only be experienced and understood by those that have come out of darkness. It can not be described, only experienced; and comparing the Bible with the Koran is just like that!

But most muslims haven't got the opportunity to experience this for themselves as they can not get their hands on a copy of the Scriptures, the Bible. Even if they can their spiritual blindness and the warnings of the Koran, make the right approach of muslims towards the Bible and the ability to receive the truth from God virtually impossible.

The Koran warns, for example: "*And will hear much that is hurtful from those to whom the Scriptures were given before you* ". (Sura 3:186 D) apart from the verses that accuse the Jews and Christians of tampering with their Scriptures.

Note: Allah is so afraid of the truth the Bible teaches and reveals, that can set people free from their slavery and misery, that he forbids the Bible in all countries where he is in control (the predominantly islamic countries; as well as in otherwise satanically controlled nations like those under a communist ideology; or even those under the control of the Roman Catholic 'church', which even burnt the translators of the Bible into the common language of the people at the stake!).

And if satan cannot cause the Bible to be forbidden in a nation, he keeps them from reading it, by keeping them busy and occupied with the pleasures of life, or with the pursuit of career, money, or even by keeping people worried and busy with the necessities of life; or by blinding them spiritually (Matthew 6:33; Matthew 13; Mark 4; Luke 8).

Satan does the same with a book like this.

Chapter Eight

Islamic society versus the Kingdom of God

Much can be learned about the nature of Allah, by viewing Islamic society as prescribed in the Koran. (notice that I did not say "as we see around us." Because muslims may do quite a different thing than what Allah says in the Koran, and it would not be fair to judge Islam and Allah by looking at such muslims.)

On the other hand, much can be learned about the nature of God by viewing the Kingdom of God as written in the Word of God, the Bible. (In line with my earlier comment, notice also here that I do not say "as we see around us." But as "written in the Word of God, the Bible." Because looking at those who may call themselves Christians but do NOT live according to the Word of God, would also give the wrong idea of the Kingdom of God. To judge Christianity by those who do not obey the Word of God, even when they are called Christians -when they do not obey the Word of God it is obvious that they are NOT Christians at all- would not be fair.

Yet, muslims keep dishonestly painting Christianity black before their islamic audience, by pointing to all the evils in the Western society, saying "Look what these Christians do!" "What a corrupt religion Christianity must be!" When they know full well that those who practise such things are no Christians, because the Word of God itself condemns such evils, and says that those who do those things will not inherit the Kingdom of God! Muslims intentionally use this dishonest argument to arouse hostility against Christianity in their islamic audience.

I do not do so but I consider Allah, not by looking at muslims but at the Koran, and I consider God, by not looking at Christians, but at the Word of God, the Bible.) I do this far too brief to do justice to the subject of Islamic society as well as to the subject of the Kingdom of

God. There is no room for that here. The only object that I have in the framework of this book, is to show that Allah and God are different, even seen from a brief overview of Islamic Society and the kingdom of God.

* In the matter of evil and sin, the views of Allah and God are totally different:

To Allah 'evil' is only that which he declared "haram" (unlawful). Allah declared it good and not evil, for example, that Mohammed's adopted son divorced his wife so that Mohammed, who had expressed his attraction to her, could marry her. And Mohammed did marry her. God, on the other hand says: "*I hate divorce!*" (Malach 2:16 NIV) Jesus said: "*Whoever divorces his wife and marries another commits adultery; and whoever marries her who is divorced from her husband commits adultery.*" (Luke 16:18)

To God evil is that which is evil in itself. In the West and Western laws the understanding of what is evil in principle still very much concurs with that which is evil in God's sight: the Biblical understanding of evil. This is because the laws in the West very much used to be based on evil as revealed in the Bible. Even when Western society has in majority turned it's back on God, the people's understanding of what is evil is still very much rooted in God's view of evil as declared by the Bible, in contrast to the islamic's society's view of evil.

* In the matter of justice Allah and God are totally different:

Let us for example consider the next passage of Scripture: "*Now there was a famine in the days of David for three years, year after year; and David inquired of the Lord. And the Lord answered, It is because of Saul and and his bloodthirsty house, because he killed the Gibeonites. So the king called the Gibeonites and spoke to them. Now the Gibeonites were not of the children of Israel, but of the remnant of the Amorites; the children of Israel had sworn protection to them, but Saul had sought to kill them in his zeal for the children of Israel and Judah.*" (2 Samuel 21:1,2 NKJV)
So God gave a famine which is, the land had incurred His curse (See Deuteronomy 28) by the bloodshed of king Saul, which was a breach of

48

the treaty that Israel had made with the Gibeonites who had tricked them to enter into this treaty (see Joshua 9), and though Israel was tricked into this for trusting their own insight and understanding rather than to inquire of God, thus displeasing and disobeying God, God now was displeased because they had broken the treaty. And therefore He had brought a famine over the land. And not until atonement was made for Saul's killing, God again heeded the prayer for the land. (See 2 Samuel 1-14) So, God proves to be a very just God. Even though Israel was His chosen people and He had ordered Israel to drive out all the people of the promised land and slay them, among whom were the Gibeonites, He later did not approve of their killing of the Gibeonites with whom the Israelites had entered into a treaty with against the will of God! Gód's justice makes no exception for His people! God in no wise shows any partiality!

Allah, on the other hand, says for example, "*Proclaim a woeful punishment to the unbelievers, except to those idolaters who have honoured their treaties with you in every detail and aided none against you. With these keep faith, until their treaties have run their term. Allah loves the righteous. When the sacred months are over slay the idolaters* (those with whom the treaties were made) *wherever you find them. Arrest them, besiege them, and lie in ambush everywhere for them.*" (Sura 9:4,5 D)
This verse is claimed to have cancelled no less than 124 verses that call for tolerance, forbearance and patience.

*Love and hatred.

In the matter of attitudes towards those outside of their respective 'societies', Allah and God are totally different:

Jesus taught: "*You have heard it was said, 'You shall love your neighbour and hate your enemy.' But I say to you, love your enemies, bless those who curse you, do good to those who hate you, and pray for those who spitefully use you and persecute you, that you may be sons of your Father in heaven; for He makes His sun rise on the evil and on the good, and sends rain on the just and on the unjust. For if you love those who love you, what reward have you? Do not even the tax collectors to the same? And if you greet your brethren only, what do you do more*

*than others? Do not even the tax collectors do so? Therefore you shall
be perfect, just as your Father in heaven is perfect."* (Matthew 5:43-48)

Allah says: *"O believers, take not Jews and Christians as your friends;
they are friends of each other. (???) Whoso of you makes them his
friends is one of them."* (that is, he is an infidel! Sura 5:56 A) *"Believers
, do not make friends with any but your own people. (muslims) They
will spare no pains to corrupt you. They desire nothing but your ruin.
Their hatred is evident from what they utter with their mouths, but
greater is the hatred which their breasts conceal."* (Sura 3:118 D)

The words of Jesus I just quoted show it is quite the opposite. An
enormous hatred against all non-muslims is evident from the verses of
the Koran! Allah even calls the Jewish religious leaders "satans.' (Sura
2:13 A) Allah also calls Jews and Christians "perverse!" (Sura 9 :30 D)

Worse yet, Allah says: *"You shall not kill any man whom Allah has
forbidden you to kill, **except for a just cause.**"* (Sura 17:32 D) A just
cause is not described, so a just cause can easily be found to justify a
killing. *"Believers, retaliation is decreed for you in bloodshed."* (Sura
2:178) *"The unbelievers are your inveterate enemies." "Seek out your
enemies relentlessly."* (Sura 4:102,104 D) *"Fight against them until
idolatry is no more and Allah's religion reigns supreme."* (Sura 2:193
D) *"Fighting is obligatory for you, much as you dislike it."* (Sura 2:216
D) This is literal physical fighting. *"Fight valiantly for his cause"* (Sura
5:35 D) *"Fight against such of those to whom the Scriptures were given
as believe neither in Allah nor in the last day, who do not forbid what
Allah and his apostle have forbidden, and do not embrace the true faith
(islam), until they pay tribute out of hand and are utterly subdued."*
(Sura 9:29 D) *"If you do not fight, he (Allah) will punish you sternly. "*
(Sura 9:39 D) *"Believers, make war on the infidels who dwell around
you. Deal firmly with them. Know that Allah is with the righteous."*
(Sura 9:123 D)

**It is not these harsh, aggressive, intolerant, hate-provoking verses
that are cancelled,** but these verses have cancelled and replaced verses
of the beginning of the appearance of Mohammed when he still sought
to be recognized and accepted by Jews and Christians and be their
spiritual leaders as well. After they rejected him as a prophet, and after

he had found the solution in Abraham's faith (see chapter 4), Mohammed did not need their recognition any longer, turned his back on them and came with these many verses of aggression against them.

These verses still stand. And wherever muslims are in power they are executed. Wherever they are not in power they seek to convince those in power of their good intentions by pointing to the verses of tolerance that have been cancelled, but that is not known to most outsiders. And thus muslims have been able to deceive many (because of the nature and character of the Westerners).

Christians are certainly called to fight, but that is not a physical fight, but a spiritual fight as mentioned in 2 Corinthians 10:3-6, of which this book is an example. The Word of God, the Bible, also says, "*Put on the whole armour of God, that you may be able to stand against the wiles of the devil. For we do not wrestle against flesh and blood, but against principalities, against powers, against the rulers of the darkness of this age, against spiritual hosts of wickedness in the heavenly places.*" (Ephesians 6;11,12)

The killing and murdering of opponents of islam is not only valued as legal, it is considered morally just, as it furthers the cause of islam. Therefore Mohammed considered his present time -poets, and - intellectuals his worst enemies. The same can be seen with other dictatorships and ideologies, like that of communism.

Therefore, where Jesus Christ commands His people to love their enemies, **Allah in the Koran incites muslims to hatred, violence, murder and war**. *In doing so the Koran violates anti-incitement-laws in probably all non-islamic nations!*

Allah tolerates no other society but Islam, and is in

constant war with all other societies. Until Islam is established there can be no lasting peace with non-islamic nations. And in the hearts of the muslims in the West and in other non-islamic nations, where they are not in control but form a minority, they utterly abhor and reject the societies and cultures etc. of their host-nations.

The Western idea of integration of muslims in their Western host nations, shows little insight in Islam by the Western governments!

The words of Allah in the Koran incite a hatred in the hearts of the muslims against their host-nations, and a violence that is always smoldering in the hearts of muslims, like a sleeping volcano, ready to erupt when triggered.

When muslims are squeezed, hatred and violence erupt, including in their language. When true Christians are squeezed, the love of Christ and the fruits of the Spirit are still seen, even more evident in the light of the pressures!

*In **the attitude towards women and towards divorce, Allah and God again are totally different:**

Allah in the Koran allows for easy, unlimited divorces. Worse yet, "*If you wish to replace a wife with another, do not take from her the dowry you have given her even if it be a talent of gold. That would be improper and grossly unjust; for how can you take it back when you have lain with each other and entered a firm contract?* " (Sura 4:20 D) So to take her dowry away from her is unjust, but not to put her away and replace her, exchanging her for another.

With what are called unbelieving women this is not even so, "*Do not hold on to your marriages with unbelieving women: demand the dowries you have given them.*" (Sura 60:11 D)

Islam teaches from Sura 4:3 that a man is allowed to marry two, three or four women. An unlimited amount of concubines are allowed, but moreover, the maximum of four wives is only at any given time. As wives can be exchanged easily, actually an unlimited amount of wives, which is, an unlimited polygamy is the reality in islam.

The only requirement is that all wives are being treated equal. Yet the Koran also says "*Try as you may, you cannot treat all your wives impartially.*" (Sura 4:129 D)

52

Divorce according to the Koran is done by three times pronouncing, by the husband - the other way around, 'of course' is not possible - the formula 'I divorce you' three times. "*If a man divorces his wife, he cannot remarry her until she has wedded another man and be divorced by him; in which case it shall be no offence for either of them to return to the other.*" (Sura 2:230 D)

The Koran also says: "*It may well be that, if he* (Mohammed) d*ivorce you* (his wives), *his lord will give him in your place better wives than yourselves, submissive to Allah and full of faith, devout, penitent, obedient, and given to fasting; both formerly-wedded and virgins.*" (Sura 66: 5 D)

Women in Islam can therefore never be sure of their husband; will he divorce them or not? They better obey him and do everything to please him!

Islam even knows a marriage for one night! This *'zawag al moutaa'* as it is called in Arabic, meaning 'marriage of pleasure,' was originally created and instituted for travelling men.

What is the difference between this one-night marriage and prostitution? A major one: A marriage is a covenant, to last until death, but a one night-'marriage' is a covenant made and broken so easily. **Showing that promises and covenants of Allah and of muslims can not be trusted!**

The attitude of Allah towards women in the Koran is already clear from "*Women are your fields: go, then into your fields whence you please.*" (Sura 2:223 D) In other words: Women are a man's possession to do with as he pleases!

Another Sura says: "*Men have authority over women* (Arberry tranlsated it with "*Men are the managers of the affairs of women*") *because Allah has made the one superior to the other, and because they spend their wealth to maintain them. Good women are obedient. .. As for those from whom you fear disobedience* (the man only has to be suspicious of it; whether it is true or not does not matter to Allah; that is another example of Allah's idea of justice.), *admonish them and send*

*them to beds apart (in other words, deny them sex with you) and **beat
them.** Then if they obey you, take no further action against them."* (Sura
4:34 D)

*"Women shall with justice have rights similar to those exercised
against them, although men have a status above women."* (Sura 2:228
D)

Ghazali, the greatest of all muslim scholars said: *"Marriage is a kind
of slavery, for the woman is subdued to her husband and it is her duty
to obey him totally, in everything that he demands of her, unless it is
against the laws of Islam."*

In Islamic society women are veiled and kept in seclusion.

Abdel al-Mar'a wrote: *"In Islam, the man has robbed the woman of all
her human attributes, and limited her to one function, namely to please
with her body...the man is an oppressor in his own house."* He
continues by calling for muslims to follow the example of the European
nations, *"where the status of the woman has been elevated to a high
level of respect and freedom of thinking and acting."*

I am sad to have to remark that he should know better. This is wishful
thinking that can never become reality in Islam because of the words of
Allah concerning women in the Koran!

In Islamic society sexual relationships are dominated by male impulses,
and jealousy is one of the strongest of these. Kazem Daghestani
says,"Jealousy of the husband comes forth from his pride and family-
honor, and not so much from love. His wife is his *'ird* -his honour. It is
his honour that is hurt if his wife would misbehave."

A recent 1999-documentary showed the incredible practice in Jordan of
women who had been raped, being murdered by their brother or other
family member, to save the family honour as in islamic society the
woman is always held guilty as she must have seduced the man to rape
her.... Such men hardly receive any punishment as the murder was to
save the family honour. This practice is not only known in Jordan. One
woman in the documentary who had incredibly survived the many

bullets that went through her is now imprisoned for life. So called to protect her, because the moment she would set foot outside the prison the family member is ready to murder her and finish of the job.

In Pakistan it's the women who were raped who are prosecuted and punished, nót the men!

But the world is silent - WORSE: GIVES BILLIONS of USD or Euros in so called human aid - as good relations between islamic nations and the West are deemed more important to the West (the lust for money being the root of all evil, as Apostle Paul wrote!) than justice and righteousness. God will visit the West in judgement for this and other evils!

Jealousy is a tradition amongst us, says Fadela M'rabet, possibly Algeria's most well known female journalist. Men are very suspicious towards women. They have the opinion that women have strong sexual instincts that they don't know to control. That is why they need to be guarded very carefully; if not than they might soon ashamed their fathers, brothers, and husbands. So, it is just that they are isolated, except for other women. Morroe Berger believes that " male suspicion towards the female sexuality probably is the counterpart of the great importance that man attach to their own sexual potential. Though men are proud of their own sexual abilities, they have to watch out, or they become the victims of the potency of other men through their wives, and unmarried daughters and sisters". The emphasis on male potency corresponds with the child-marriages, polygamy and easy divorce conditions for the male. Though the polygamy recently and especially in the large cities and with more developed people, has diminished strongly, the sanctity of the sexual potency of the man is sustained and strengthens the unsatisfied male lust in such a way that eroticism has become an obsession
.

Fadela M'rabet who had to emigrate to France, to be able to continue working as publicist, often writes embittered and with frustration about the separation in a male and female society in Algeria. By telling women what they are not allowed to do, to wear, to read, to watch, to love, without making clear what they can become, she says, the men are blocking off all progress, and thus they perpetuate and affirm the confusion, hatred, the sectarianism and prejudges that already exist.

Also the Lebanese journalist G'hadah al-Samman complains about male attitudes. *"In present Arabic society we have to conclude that the chastity belt is still forced upon the women, to her spirit just as much as to her body- if not stronger. A woman who shows frankness and boldness of thinking and speech, will receive much more rejection and disapproval, than the prostitute who will never get herself into such a situation. "*

If Islamic society already looks like hell on earth for the muslim-woman, how much greater hell will Islamic Paradise be to her!

Islamic Paradise is a sensual place in which male lusts are catered for! He can drink from rivers of wine and eat his belly full; but most of all, have unlimited sex with an unlimited amount of "high-bosomed maidens", " dark-eyed houris", "bashful virgins", ""bashful dark-eyed virgins", "boys with eternal youth", (throughout the Koran).

Islamic Paradise reveals a lot about Allah's morals! Especially since Allah is said to immediately reward those who die 'in the cause of Allah, the so called 'shahadas' who blow themselves up in the middle of innocent citizens, and in fact are murderers! But then so are Allah, satan, and Mohammed!

However, the people who went to hell and/or heaven, as we can learn from their testimonies in www.spiritlessons.com NEVER saw Mohammed in heaven; well, they did not see Mohammed, period! They ONLY saw Jesus Christ!

So why do muslims want to continue to follow a dead man with such evil character-traits, who constantly seeks forgiveness from Allah in the Koran, instead of the LIVING Christ, Who rose from the dead, and who NEVER SINNED, and has shown His perfect character. Who gave Himself in death, suffering for us, paying the penalty for our sins. When Mohammed only enjoyed the pleasures of his life, and was utterly selfish, and showed to be very short-tempered!

56

Much more can be said about the position of women in Islamic society of which the Koran says: "*You are the noblest nation that has ever been raised up for mankind. You enjoy justice and forbid evil. You believe in Allah.*" (Sura 3:110 D)

I leave it up to the reader to decide if this is so. This is sufficient to see who Allah is and that he is totally different from God

How different is God's attitude towards women, and towards fornication, adultery, divorce and all other unrighteousness and sin, as revealed in the Bible, from that of Allah as revealed in the Koran! In comparing Allah's response to Mohammed's desire to marry the wife of his adopted son, Zayd, and how God responded to David's adultery with Bathsheba, the vast difference between Allah and God can be seen.

Furthermore Jesus Christ said: "*I say to you that whoever looks at a woman to lust for her has already committed adultery with her in his heart.*" (Matthew 5:28) In Jesus Christ "*there is neither male nor female; for you* (who are in Christ) *are all one in Christ Jesus.*" (Galatians 3:28)
God hates divorce! (Malachi 2:16 NIV)

Jesus Christ said: "*Whoever divorces his wife and marries another commits adultery; and whoever marries her who is divorced from her husband commits adultery.*" (Luke 16:18; also Mattew 5:32 and 19:9, and Mark 10:11,12)

Jesus said: "*For out of the heart proceed evil thoughts, murders, adulteries, fornications, thefts, false witness, blasphemies. These are the things which defile a man, but to eat with unwashed hands does not defile a man.*" (Matthew 15:19,20; also Mark 7:21 which also mentions: "*covetousness, wickedness, deceit, lewdness, an evil eye, pride, foolishness.*")

Jesus spoke here to his disciples about the scribes and Pharisees, the religious leaders of His time, who made the command of God of no effect by their tradition. He had just told the religious leaders: "*Hypocrites! Well did Isaiah prophesy about you, saying, 'These people draw near to Me with their mouth, and honour Me with their lips, but their heart is far from Me. And in vain they worship Me, teaching as doctrines the commandments of men.*" His disciples the told Jesus Christ: "*Do you know that the Pharisees were offended when they heard this saying?*" (Matthew 15:7-9; 12)

For fear of being accused of publishing things offensive to the Jewish religious teachers, the present-day 'Politically-Correct' Western media would probably have censured Jesus Christ's words! It shows how humanistic, how stupid, and how utterly in just Western society has become!

God also says of the kingdom of God: "*Do you not know that the unrighteous will not inherit the kingdom of God? Do not be deceived. Neither fornicators, nor idolaters, not adulterers, nor homosexuals, nor sodomites, nor thieves, nor covetous, nor drunkards, nor revilers, nor extortionors will inherit the kingdom of God.*" (1 Corinthians 6:9,10)

"*Now the works of the flesh are evident, which are: adultery, fornication, uncleanness, lewdness, idolatry, sorcery, hatred, contentions, jealousies, outbursts of wrath, selfish ambitions, dissensions, heresies, envy, murders, drunkenness, revelries, and the like; of which I tell you beforehand, just as I told you in time past, that those who practice such things will not inherit the kingdom of God. But the fruit of the Spirit is love, joy, peace, longsuffering, kindness, goodness, faithfulness, gentleness, self-control. Against such there is no law. And those who are Christ's have crucified the flesh with its passions and desires.*" (Galatians 5:19-24)

"*Flesh and blood cannot inherit the kingdom of God; nor does corruption inherit incorruption.*" (1 Corinthians 15:50)

"*Your throne, O God, is forever and ever; a scepter of righteousness is the scepter of Your kingdom. You have loved righteousness and hated lawlessness.*" (Hebrews 1:8, 9a) "*the kingdom which He promised to those who love Him.*" (James 2:5b)

In contrast to the sensual nature of Islamic Paradise, Jesus told the Sadducees (a Jewish religious sect which did not believe in the resurrection): "*You are mistaken, not knowing the Scriptures nor the power of God. For in the resurrection they neither marry nor are given in marriage, but are like angels of God in heaven. But concerning the resurrection of the dead, have you not read what was spoken to you by God, saying, 'I am the God of Abraham, the God of Isaac, and the God of Jacob?' God is not a God of the dead, but of the living.*" (Matthew 22:23-32) In the resurrection we will not have this body of flesh, but we will have a glorified body!

Jesus Christ when he was captured by the Jewish religious leaders, and put in front of the Roman governor of Palestine, Pilate, said: "*My kingdom is not of this world. If My kingdom were of this world, My servants would fight, so that I should not be delivered to the Jews; but now My kingdom is not from here.*" (John 18: 36)

Therefore Christians should not give in to the temptation to establish the kingdom of God on earth by human means, in human power. The Roman Catholic church with their "Civitate Dei," (City of God concept) tried this.

Allah on the other hand wants the whole world to become part of the 'daar-al-islam,' "the house of Islam." And until then, nations who are not part of it, are part of the 'daar-al-harb,' that is, "nations where Islam is not yet established, and whith which Allah is in a state of war!" Allah wants to establish his Islamic society therefore by means of violance.

How different God wants to establish His Kingdom. Jesus Christ told Nicodemus, a Pharisee and ruler of the Jews who came to Him by night, "*Most assuredly, I say to you, unless one is born again, he cannot see the kingdom of God,*" and "*Most assuredly, I say to you, unless one is born of water and the Spirit, he cannot enter the kingdom of God. That which is born of the flesh is flesh, and that which is born of the Spirit is spirit.*" (John 3: 3,5,6; I will explain how the reader can be born again, of the Spirit of God, in the last chapter of this book.)

"*The Kingdom of God is not eating and drinking, but righteousness and peace and joy in the Holy Spirit.*" (Romans 14:17)

59

How far far different Islamic society as well as Islamic Paradise are! *"The kingdom of God is not in word but in power."* (1 Corinthians 4:20)

Jesus teaches many more things on the kingdom of God, but this suffices to show that **Allah as viewed from Islamic society and Islamic Paradise, as Allah says in the Koran, is so totally different from God, as viewed from the Kingdom of God as revealed in the Bible, the Word of God.**

One last word on the kingdom of God is that *"we,* disciples of Jesus Christ, *must through many tribulations enter the kingdom of God."* (Acts 14:22)

Life for the true Christian is not an easy life! Scripture also says that *"all who desire to live godly in Christ Jesus will suffer persecution."* (2 Timothy 3:12)

But God has given the Christian many promises of His comfort, His care, His healing, answered prayers, peace that passes all understanding, etc.

A very important thing I want to mention here, is **the difference in God's way of dealing with sin, and Allah's way of dealing with it .**

Through Moses God gave the Law to His chosen people Israel, and covenanted with them. The book of Hebrews in the New Testament speaks of a new covenant, and of our High Priest Jesus Christ, who was made priest with an oath by Him who said to Him: *"The lord has sworn and will not relent, You are a priest forever according to the order of Melchizedek. "* (Hebrews 7:21; Psalm 110: 4)

"For such a High Priest was fitting for us, who is holy, harmless, undefiled, separate from sinners, and has become higher than the heavens; who does not need daily, as those high priests, to offer up sacrifices, first for his own sins and then for the people's, for this He did once for all when He offered up Himself. For the law appoints as high priests men who have weakness, but the word of the oath, which came after the law, appoints the Son who has been perfected forever." (Hebrews 7: 26-28)

And God says that *"if that first covenant had been faultless, then no place would have been sought for a second. Because finding fault with them, He says: 'Behold the days are coming, says the Lord, when I will make a new covenant with the house of Israel and with the house of Judah - not according to the covenant that I made with their fathers in the day when I took them by the hand to lead them out of the land of Egypt; because they did not continue in My covenant, and I disregarded them, says the Lord. For this is the covenant that I will make with the house of Israel after those days, says the Lord: I will put My laws in their mind and write them on their hearts; and I will be their God, and they shall be My people. None of them shall teach his neighbour, and none his brother, saying, 'Know the Lord,' for all shall know Me, from the least of them to the greatest of them. For I will be merciful to their unrighteousness, and their sins and their lawless deeds I will remember no more.' In that He says, 'A new covenant, He has made the first obsolete. Now what is becoming obsolete and growing old is ready to vanish away."* (Hebrews 8:7-13)

The first covenant was dedicated by Moses with the blood of calves and goats, the second covenant with the blood of Jesus Christ. (Hebrews 9:16-28) *"For it is not possible that the blood of bulls and goats could take away sins."* (Hebrews 10: 4) *"Previously saying, 'Sacrifice and offerings, burnt offerings, and offerings for sin You did not desire, nor had pleasure in them '* (Psalm 40: 6 -8) *(which are offered according to the law), then He said, 'Behold, I have come to do your will, O God.' He takes away the first that He may establish the second. By that will we have been sanctified through the offering of the body of Christ once for all. And every priest stands ministering daily and offering repeatedly the same sacrifices, which can never take away sins. But this Man, after He had offered one sacrifice for sins forever, sat down at the right hand of God, from that time waiting till His enemies are made His footstool. For by one offering He has perfected forever those who are being sanctified. But the Holy Spirit also witnesses to us; for after He had said before, 'This is the covenant that I will make with them after those days, says the Lord: 'I will put My laws into their hearts, and in their minds I will write them, then He adds, 'Their sins and their lawless deeds I will remember no more.'* (Jeremiah 31: 33,34) *Now where there is remission of these, there is no longer an offering for sin."* (Hebrews 10: 8 - 18)

God had commanded His people Israel through Moses His servant:
*"Hear, O Israel: The Lord our God, the Lord is one! You shall love the
Lord your God with all your heart, with all your soul, and with all your
strength. And these words which I command you today shall be in your
heart. You shall teach them diligently to your children, and shall talk of
them when you sit in your house, when you walk by the way, when you
lie down, and when you rise up. You shall bind them as a sign on your
hand, and they shall be as frontlets between your eyes. You shall write
them on the doorposts of your house and on your gates."* (Deuteronomy
6: 4-9)

In contrast to the new covenant where God puts His laws in our hearts
and minds, the old covenant required man to do this himself. That is
why it failed. Jesus Christ told the Jewish religious leaders of His day:
*"Well did Isaiah prophesy of you hypocrites, as it is written: 'This
people honors Me with their lips, but their heart is far from Me."* (Mark
7: 6)

God is not interested in His people's outward compliance with His law!
He wants their heart, soul and mind! That is why under the new
covenant, which is already in force dedicated with the blood of Jesus
Christ Himself, and activated in the born-again Christian, God Himself
puts His laws into our hearts and minds, by His Spirit.

Jesus Christ said *"Do not think that I came to destroy the Law or the
Prophets. I did not come to destroy but to fulfil."* (Matthew 5: 17) Jesus
Christ sharpened the Law. He said, for example: *"You have heard that
it was said to those of old, 'You shall not commit adultery.'* (Exodus 20:
14; Deuteronomy 5: 18) *But I say to you that whoever looks at a
woman to lust for her has already committed adultery with her in his
heart."* (Matthew 5:27,28)

If things are so, is there any hope for us? Yes there is! In Christ Jesus
God dealt with both the consequences of sin as well as with the power
of sin. Having done that, He gives His new creations in Christ Jesus (2
Corinthians 5:17) His Holy Spirit to all who ask Him. (Luke 11:9-13;
Matthew 3: 11,12; Luke 3:16; John 7: 38,39; 20:22; Acts 1:8; Acts 2: 4,

38) "*For whom He foreknew, He also predestined to be conformed to the image of His Son, that He might be the firstborn among many brethren.*" (Romans 8:29; 2 Corinthians 3: 18) "*I beseech you therefore, brethren, by the mercies of God, that you present your bodies a living sacrifice, holy, acceptable to God, which is your reasonable service. And do not be conformed to this world, but be transformed by the renewing of your mind, that you may prove what is that good and acceptable and perfect will of God.*" (Romans 12:1,2)

So, this is God's way of dealing with sin. In Jesus Christ He saves us and delivers us from the consequences and the power of sin, and then He changes us from the inside out into the image of Jesus Christ, by His Spirit. Because the law was no able to do that!

In Islam, on the other hand, Allah again produced an outward law, which cannot even begin to compare with God's law given through Moses! And which we know cannot change people. Muslims are required to perform the "*rites of worship*" prescribed in the Koran. (Sura 2:127 D) Like programmed robots. In Islam the solution to the problem of evil is by totalitarian outward control of every aspect of existence in islamic society. Muslims have to outwardly submit to the islamic laws. In their hearts they may feel to do quite different things, but they are restricted in their freedom by the islamic laws to act out what is in their hearts. The evil nature of the heart of man is not dealt with in Islam. Therefore if the restrictions and Islamic control fall away because the muslim moves to a non-islamic nation, he may become worse than beasts, doing what he wants to do, restricted only by what he can get away with legally.

Islam's ideal society is an islamic state with islamic law that dictates all subjects in a super-totalitarian way (it's the worst kind when a higher being is referred to that is said to order and/or justify all that is being done), denying all individual expression, and freedom to everyone!

God changes society by changing people from the inside out. But He can and will only change those people who have become His children by being born-again by the Spirit of God, by their personal choice and will. God has given every individual this freedom of choice. The freedom God gave mankind, carries great responsibilities, and great risks. God did not give the individuals their freedom so they might become and act like devils. But God created man and gave him a free will out of necessity: love demands it; for love cannot exist in an environment controlled by force! God wants men and women to freely choose to love Him! When people choose this, He can transform them through the process that makes them into the image of Jesus Christ, after He made them a new creation supernaturally by His Spirit when they were born-again! (2 Corinthians 5:17; Romans 8:29; 2 Corinthians 3:18) Freedom in a society only works with people who choose to act morally and responsibly! If people refuse this, laws become necessary! As well as the enforcement of them. But this is NOT the way of the kingdom of God.

Scripture says of those who have the fruit of the Spirit grown and developed in them: "*Against such there is no law.*" (Galatians 5:23) Reason is because they already act lawfully by nature. *"Knowing this: that the law is not made for a righteous person, but for the lawless and subordinate, for the ungodly and the sinners, for the unholy and profane, for murderers of fathers and murderers of mothers, for manslayers* (that Allah commands muslims in the Koran to be!), *for fornicators, for sodomites, for kidnappers, for liars, for perjurers, and if there is anything that is contrary to sound doctrine, according to the glorious gospel of the blessed God which was committed to my trust."* (1 Timothy 1: 9-11)

The liberty that God gave every individual of mankind carries the risk of being abused. As Westerners in majority have chosen to turn their backs on God, and become a law unto themselves, doing what they feel like doing, the West becomes more and more occult and pagan, *"for rebellion,"* Scripture says, *"is as the sin of witchcraft. And stubbornness is as iniquity and idolatry."* (1 Samuel 15:23)

But because Islam does nót change the heart of man, and because Islam denies people all freedom, the risk of evil still deserves preference above a totalitarian dictatorship of Islam. Because that is no solution to evil at all; at best it suppresses evil.

The weakness of Islam to deal with sin is shown for example in how it deals with lust: Muslim women have to cover up all of their body, so that male lust is not aroused. Clearly then the muslim has not at all conquered his lust by this. The person who can look at a woman without lusting for her, and without her having covered herself as a muslim woman, has conquered it; at least to a normal human level that does not dictate women to go dressed like that. Western men, especially European men, therefore behave more naturally and respectfully with women than muslims. Muslims who come to the West, or meet Western women do not know how to behave properly.

The sexual code, according to Dr. Sania Hamady, is so strict and limiting that an Arabic man, when he is alone with a woman, makes sexual advances. According to Fadela M'rabet many a muslim that has been gripped by sexual possession interprets social progress in terms of licentiousness. "Thus a woman who passes freely becomes 'defiant', a friendly smile of a women, 'an invitation', and a charming appearance 'licentious'. Thus not only Western women are put on a level with whores, but also all Algerian women that behave somewhat modern."

By giving themselves over to such phantasies, reasons Miss M'rabet, the men get rid of their obsession while they don't violate their conscience; they feel justified for locking up their sisters while they chase the sisters of their neighbours, for those neighbour girls are 'bad maids'.

Many Western women have become victims of muslim men, because they did not know how muslim men thought and felt. And because the Western governments refused to inform the West, and because they were and are more interested in their programme of integration of muslims in Western society, when they should know full well that by definition muslims can never integrate into Western or any society apart from Islam! Muslims, instructed by the Koran, will always be hostile to all societies outside of Islam!

The hypocrisy is that Islamic religious leaders continuously accuse the Christians of all the evils of the so called 'Christian' West,' in their attempt to paint the darkest picture of Christianity they possibly can. (They don't care if their arguments are not fair and honest; as long as it serves Islam, everything is allowed!) This method was also used by the communists to paint Western society as evil and as dark as they possibly could, denying at the same time their people access to information from the west itself! When a system needs to do that to survive, it shows how utterly weak it is!

By the way, if Islam is the best and " noblest nation that has ever been raised up for mankind" (Sura 3: 106 D), how come millions of muslims deny that and witness to the very opposite with their feet by emigrating to the West, even to those very nations they were colonised by? Why, if Islam is the "best society ever brought forth to men," do so many millions of muslims move to the 'inferior' Western nations? Is it not that with their very feet millions of muslims vote and testify to the fact that they think the West is a better society than their Islamic nations of origin! Don't these millions of muslims testify with their feet to the fact that they think the Koran is wrong? Because their feet are saying that Islam is NOT the best society raised up for mankind; otherwise they would stay there!

Chapter Nine

Allah punishes people by transforming them into apes and swine

God never changes people into animals

"Say: 'People of the Book, is it not that you hate us only because we believe in Allah and in what has been revealed to us and to others before, and because most of you are evil-doers?' Say:' Shall I tell you who will receive a worse reward from Allah? Those whom Allah has cursed and with whom he has been angry, transforming them into apes and swine." (Sura 5:60 D)

"You have heard of those of you (Israelites) that broke the Sabbath. We (Allah) said to them: 'You shall be changed into detested apes.' We made their fate an example to their own generation and to those who followed them, and a lesson to the righteous." (Sura 2: 65 D)

God does not change people, whom He originally created in His image (Genesis 1:26,27) into apes and swine, the image of beasts.

Chapter Ten

Revelation of God in the Bible &

in the lives of people throughout the ages

compared to Allah who revealed himself only to Mohammed

God revealed Himself to Adam, Eve, Enoch, Noah, Abraham, Isaäc, Jacob renamed Israel, Joseph, Moses, the people of Israel, David, Solomon, and to many others. They knew Him from firsthand experience! He gave His Word, the Bible through inspiration by the Holy Spirit, inspiring His chosen servants, Moses, David, Solomon, the prophets, His chosen apostles Peter, John. Paul, Jesus' brothers James and Jude, the tax collector Matthew, the doctor Luke, etc. God has also revealed Himself in many other ways to His people. He revealed Himself in the miracles that He performed before His people Israel, and in the law He gave them. He revealed Himself through His nation Israel and through the prophets, and finally He revealed Himself through His Son. Since the outpouring of the Holy Spirit over the 120 disciples (including Mary, mother of Jesus.), which event marked the beginning of the church in Jerusalem, God reveals Himself mainly by His Spirit in and through the church, the Body of Christ. Not just in word but in power, in miracles, healings, deliverances, salvations etc. etc. of many people **to this very day. God reveals Himself this way, in and through the church, the Body of Christ, every day!**

Nowadays Jesus Christ also appears to many muslims in a dream or vision! Speaking to them, telling them He is Jesus, and they must follow Him. Watch testimonies on www.youtube.com/muslims4jesus

When Mohammed was asked why there were no miracles confirming his calling as a messenger from Allah, he only pointed to the Koran as the miracle. But even the Koran had not been written when Mohammed died.

Allah never 'revealed' himself to anyone but to one person by the name of Mohammed. It is therefore amazing (this may be the 'miracle' but rather is showing the power of satan to blind so many people) that 1 billion people trust this one man's word for it, while at the same time rejecting the testimony of all the rest of God's prophets and servants, who, though they did not consult with each other, living often far apart, in both time as well as place, wrote His Word, in perfect harmony with each other, which only proves that the true author of the Bible is not these men, who merely wrote what God 'breathed' in them, but the Holy Spirit of God!

The fact that the words of one man in the Koran are not at all in harmony with the Bible, the Word of God, is good enough reason to reject this man as being inspired by God!

But Mohammed, when confronted with this, found another solution to this conflict. Not Mohammed was wrong, he maintained, no, even though he was just one man saying this to save his life and movement, all the others were wrong. They had changed the original text... This utterly arrogant, preposterous, absurd nonsense, could only survive in the desert of Arabia. If Mohammed had made such remarks in the Christian world, he would have been tried for blasphemy, inciting hatred, and division, and making a dangerous sect. And we would have never heard of him again.

How absurd this accusation by Mohammed is, can be seen when one studies the manuscript evidence for the New Testament as well as the Old. No other classic work in all of history has so much document evidence. It is absolutely impossible that any change could have been made to the text of the Bible. The whole Jewish and Christian world would have protested it.

Think what happens if any muslim or group of muslims would decided to change the text of the Koran. Could they do it, without being attacked and their false Koran's be destroyed? Now how could any muslim for one moment think that any Christian or Jewish sect could have done this, and not have been attacked, and ex-communicated by the church and their books burnt?

The burden of proof lies not with the church to prove that Mohammed's accusations are absurd, but with Mohammed.

But he never said what was changed in the Bible and when it was changed and by whom it was changed. Yet this accusation is enough for most muslims to reject the Bible as false and for Saudi Arabia to ban it from the nation.

How tragic! Because only the truth can set the muslims free! And if they can not find out the truth for themselves but are only brainwashed in what the people in power have decided they must believe, then there is little hope for their salvation. For **"Neither is there salvation in any other: for there is none other name under heaven given among men, whereby we must be saved,"** except the name of Jesus Christ! (Acts 4:12)

Chapter Eleven

Experiencing God compared to 'experiencing' Allah

That the Bible is the Word of God is not only evidenced by all the fulfilled prophecies which no human mind could have ever come up with, but also by the personal experiences of people who act, pray and live according to His Word, the Bible! All born-again Christians can testify of the fact that when they prayed to God, according to the Word of God, to be made a child of God, that God answered that prayer! By doing so, God proved and proves that Jesus Christ is alive, and that He does what He said He will do in the Bible! Many Christians have been healed of their diseases, when they prayed and expected according to the Bible! Many have been delivered from demons. Many have been healed of their shattered emotions and broken spirits. Many have received a joy and a peace instead of their turmoil, sadness and sorrow. Not only that, but God guides each and every true Christian by His very own Holy Spirit, personally! How vastly different are the Koran and Allah! There is no comparing!

The way God is experienced by people personally, how they experience being born again, thus becoming a new creation, with all the old passed away, how they experience a cleansing from all unrighteousness; how they experience a lifting from the burden of guilt from the sins committed as they experience God's forgiveness in Christ Jesus; how they experience to be filled with the Holy Spirit; how they experience His fellowship in His Word, in prayer and in worship , in the church, in their personal walk with Him, as He personally communicates with them, etc. is so immensely, so endlessly, so vastly different from what muslims experience of Allah!

Ex-muslim converts to Jesus Christ themselves testify how empty they felt, how restless, and how filled with all kinds of anxieties, until they accepted Jesus Christ and believed in Him according to the Bible, and invited Him in, for He says, "*Behold, I stand at the door and knock. If*

*anyone hears My voice and opens the door, I will come into him and
dine with him, and he with Me. To him who overcomes I will grant to
sit with Me on My throne, as I also overcame and sat down with My
Father on His throne.*" (Revelation 3:20,21)

The book *"Evidence That Demands A Verdict,"* by Josh McDowell,
relates the next account of the conversion of a muslim to Christ:

"Bishop John A. Subhan of the Methodist Episcopal Church at
Hyderabad was a convert from Islam. He was born in Calcutta into a
well-to-do Muslim family whose ancestors were of the Moghul race
and who had served in the Great Moghul's court. The new stage
originated in a simple event; a Muslim friend gave him a copy of the
Gospel. When the same thing had happened a few years earlier, he had
torn it to pieces in spite of an unsatisfied longing. This longing, to
know and understand the revelation given in Jesus, had never subsided.
On the contrary, his close acquaintance with Sufism had intensified it.

Now, he decided to study the book. He still considered it corrupt, but
he argued that it must contain at least parts of the original revelation.
As for its blasphemous contents, surely they could easily be detected
and discarded as interpolations or inventions of wicked Christians!
The result of his initial reading was startling. First, he did not find a
single blasphemous or satanic clause, though he had read it with
vigilance. Secondly, his common sense told him that the deliberate
corruption of sacred books must have a sufficient motive behind it. His
close examination of the Gospel yielded no adequate ground for such
an act. The high ethical teaching of the Gospel, for example, bore no
mark of tampering; there was no ethic of convenience here. He reached
the same conclusion in the study of the Gospel narratives. No disciple
would have invented the crucifixion story with its shameful treatment
of the founder of Christianity. Even if true, the crucifixion would have
been the first thing to be removed or modified. How plainly it refuted
that Jesus was the Son of God!

This wrestling of the young Muslim with his preconceived ideas of the
New Testament is revealing. His second reading of the Gospel
produced a deep conviction that it was the true *Injil*, that it was God's
word and His revelation. The effect of reading the Gospel was

markedly different from that produced by the recitation of the Quran. Upon his second reading Subhan decided to become a Christian. He was convinced that Christianity was the only true religion. The conviction and decision are remarkable, for apart from the Gospel he had no knowledge of the Christian faith. All the time he had been moving within Islam. He had no Christian friends; the Gospel was given to him by a Muslim. He sums up his experience of Christianity in these words: 'It is not a mere acceptance of certain beliefs and dogmas, though they are necessary, but essentially it is living in close fellowship with Christ. It is not a religion to be practiced, but also a life to be lived.'" Testimonies of ex-muslims: www.youtube.com/muslims4jesus

Christianity is a relationship, a fellowship with the living God, the living Christ, which is vastly more than any religion, for religions are merely attempts of humans reaching some god or 'divine' consciousness, within or without themselves, through religious practices, based on words of some person, and dubious demonic 'revelations', while Christianity is God revealing Himself in so many different ways, times, people, reaching out to man, and being continuously active, caring for His creation, and longing to see all people come to the knowledge of Jesus Christ, so that all may be saved and have fellowship with Him for eternity.

Jesus Christ is alive, as is also evidenced in the lives of all who belong to Him, while the founders of all religions are dead. Muslims visit the grave of Mohammed; the tomb of Jesus Christ is empty, because Jesus Christ rose from the dead, and ascended into heaven! From there He will return!

So Christianity is a practical living walk in fellowship with Him, while religions are attempts in human efforts by dead works, serving only the devil to keep people away from truly knowing the living God, Jesus Christ, while giving them the false idea and security that they are in the truth. Christianity is Life, religions are death.

If Christianity looses its life and turns into a religion, making the Word of God of none effect trough traditions and man-made doctrines and becoming Christianity in name only, it also keeps people from coming to a true saving knowledge of Jesus Christ. It then becomes an enemy of God, resisting His Holy Spirit, even persecuting the true disciples of Jesus Christ.

As the religious Jews murdered Jesus Christ, so these name-christians murder true Christians, even convinced they do God a favour, as the Jews thought they did in murdering Christ Jesus for blasphemy! Scripture tells it thus, *"the new covenant, not of the letter but of the Spirit; for the letter kills, but the Spirit gives life."* (2 Corinthians 3:6 NKJV) Many, many people have been killed by the letter of the Word of God abusively used, wrongly motivated; not used as the Spirit gave and taught, but after their own flesh.

Apostle John writes, *"That which was from the beginning, which we have heard, which we have seen with our eyes, which we have looked upon, and our hands have handled, concerning the Word of life- the life was manifested, and we have seen, and bear witness, and declare to you that eternal life which was with the Father and was manifested to us- that which we have seen and heard we declare to you, that you also may have fellowship with us; and truly our fellowship is with the Father and with His Son Jesus Christ. And these things we write to you that your joy may be full. This is the message which we have heard from Him and declare to you, that God is light and in Him is no darkness at all. If we say that we have fellowship with Him, and walk in darkness, we lie and do not practice the truth. But if we walk in the light as He is in the light, we have fellowship with one another, and the blood of Jesus Christ His Son cleanses us from all sin. If we say that we have no sin, we deceive ourselves, and the truth is not in us. If we confess our sins, He is faithful and just to forgive us our sins and to cleanse us from all unrighteousness. If we say that we have not sinned, we make Him a liar, and His word is not in us. My little children, these things I write to you, so that you may not sin. And if anyone sins, we have an Advocate with the Father, Jesus Christ the righteous. And He Himself is the propitiation for our sins, and not for ours only but for the whole world. Now by this we know that we know Him, if we keep His commandments. He who says, "I know Him", and does not keep His commandments, is a liar, and the truth is not in him. But whoever keeps His word, truly the love of God is perfected in him. By this we know that we are in Him. He who says he abides in Him ought himself also to walk just as He walked."* (1 John 1:1-2:6 NKJV)

74

Chapter Twelve

Summarizing

Though the Koran, as quoted at the beginning of this book (Sura 29:47), emphatically declares that Allah and God are one (when Mohammed was still convinced - because he 'borrowed' the verses from a Christian-sect and Jews – he would be accepted by them as their 'last' prophet.') , we have clearly seen now that they are not one at all, but totally different.

I explained and established that Allah and God cannot be one and the same, because:

1. Allah has no son, but God has a Son by the name of Jesus Christ; the only Name by which men can and must be saved. (Acts 4:12)

2. The background of Allah, and the way he is worshipped, prayed to, honoured is pagan. Even though he cloaked himself with some attributes of God, 'borrowing' them from God by taking them from Bible stories Mohammed had heard in twisted form, his true nature can nevertheless easily be discerned.

3. Allah is the ancient idol of Mecca, the only one Mohammed left from the 360 idols of the Ka'ba in Mecca. God, on the other hand, chose Jerusalem as His city, but has rejected her because they rejected Jesus Christ as their Messiah! God's city is the city called New Jerusalem, which will descend out of heaven from God. (Revelation 21: 9- 21)

4. God fulfils His Word. The Bible and history are full of evidences of God fulfilling prophecies He gave in His Word, the Bible, in detail! Allah did none of that in the Koran, nor is it evident in Islamic history.

5. The name 'Allah' is the contraction of 'al' which means 'the' and 'ilah' which means 'god.' 'Allah' therefore means 'the-god,' and is 'the-god' of

the Ka'ba and region of Mecca: the ancient Arabic idol. Hence Allah and God are opponents, enemies!

6. The personality, character, way of doing, etc. of Allah as seen from the Kor'an is totally different from that of God as revealed in the Bible.

7. A view of Islamic society and the Kingdom of God shows Allah and God to be totally different.

8. Allah punishes people by changing them into apes and swine; God never changes people into animals.

9.The way God has revealed and still reveals Himself, is so vastly different from the way Allah has 'revealed' himself. It is different in amount of people, the number of times, and the various ways and the times of revelation of God, during thousands of years, to this very day.

God is not silent, nor absent nor distant. He is very much alive and active and involved in His creation and in the lives of His creatures! He cares for them!

Allah is so distant that once He gave Mohammed his recitations, he was never heard of again!

In contrast to God, Allah only gave his recitations to one man, Mohammed, during a very short period of time, never confirming Mohammed with signs, wonders and miracles as God had confirmed His Word through His servants, through the prophets of old, through the apostles, through disciples like Philip (Acts 8:6-8), and still confirms His Word to and through the believers (Mark 16:17,18) to this very day!

Allah is so distant and silent that he cannot be reached by the individual muslim. All this should cause great suspicions!

Christians pray and are heard by God! He answers them, according to His promises in the Bible.

The Islamic 'salaat', practiced 5 times a day by muslims, is only a recitation of 'names' of Allah, (*3 of the 99 names of Allah are actually names of satan: The Most Proud One, the Utmost Deceiver, and The One Who Causes Death!/ the Greatest Murderer!*) and of Islamic confessions, in a prescribed formula, like a record, and it should not be confused with prayer or communication from an individual 's heart and spirit. It doesn't even really involve the muslim's mind, either.

How does Allah reveal himself in the lives of the individual muslim? Can any muslim testify that Allah revealed himself to him, as so many people testify of God? Even Mohammed never testified, nor claimed that Allah ever revealed himself to him; he always said that it was 'Gibriel' who related to him 'the words of Allah.' (It cannot have been the true archangel Gabriel, because the Koran contradicts the words of Gabriel in the Bible.)

Can the invidiual muslim testify of anything done by Allah for him personally? Yet, every born-again Christian can testify Jesus Christ made him/her a new creation in Christ Jesus! (2 Corinthians 5:17) All born - again Christians knów that God made them His child! They knów God forgave them their sins and trespasses, and gave them a supernatural peace with God that passes all understanding. They know from their individual personal experience!

10.The way God gave His Word, the Bible, is so vastly different from the way Mohammed got the recitations, that after his death were made into the Koran. More on this in my complete volume "A Christian Defence Against Accusations of Islam."

11.The way God, and Jesus Christ is experienced and has been experienced in the lives of countless numbers of people throughout the ages, is so vastly different from the way muslim 'experience' Allah (muslims don't experience Allah. They are left in the dark and do the rites as automats)

12. God fulfils His Word, His promises! God backs up His Word as revealed in the Bible; confirming His Word continually, proving that the Bible is God's Word by His continual actions, in the lives of

individuals, in the corporate life of His church, and in the world. Allah has never backed up the Koran.

Allah never backs up the Koran in any muslim's life, neither individually nor corporately, nor in the world. Allah does as he wills.

Christians call upon God according to His Word, believing that if they fulfil the conditions stated; that if they belong to Him, and are His child; and believe God to do as He is requested to do, in accordance with His promise as stated in His Word; in other words to expect God to act according to His Word, that God will do it! Jesus said *"According to your faith let it be to you."* (Matthew 9: 29) And also :*"Your faith has made you well."* (Matthew 9:22; Mark 5: 34; Mark 10: 52; Luke 7: 50; Luke 8: 48; Luke 17: 19; Luke18: 42)

Muslims have no such promises from Allah, nor do they have any expectations that Allah would ever be interested in them. To muslims Allah watches them as a bird of prey does it's prey; or as a dictator watches his subjects to see the smallest mistake or the smallest transgression to punish them. That is why muslims live in constant fear of Allah!

Yet why are there still muslims around, when things are this way? They should run to the living God: to Jesus Christ, Who also loves thém so much that he died for them too, and is so ready to meet them in every possible good way, according to His word and many good promises!

13. God is personally interested in the individual. He even knows how many hairs you have on your head! (Matthew 10:30;Luke 21:18) That means, that God is so interested in us that He even knows the smallest, most insignificant details of our lives; so how much more does He know the things that matter to us!

And God cares! He says to His own not to worry about what to eat or drink, or what to wear, " *for after all these things the Gentiles seek.*" For the heavenly Father knows that we need all these things. " *But seek first the kingdom of God and His righteousness, and all these things shall be added unto you. Therefore do not worry about tomorrow, for tomorrow will worry about its own things.* " (Matthew 6:25-34)

This vast subject of God's interest in the individual; His love; His care, even to the point of taking the form of a human being to die for mankind to save him; takes many many volumes. In the context of the subject of this book, I merely want to point out, that also in this regard God is so vastly different from Allah. Muslims do not expect Allah to be interested in them, let alone to do anything for them. They serve out of servitude, as slaves of Allah.

14. God instituted the Sabbath in the Law, even in the Ten Commandments, commanding His people Israel to keep the Sabbath holy, because in six days the Lord made the heavens and the earth, the sea, and all that is in them, and rested the seventh day. (Exodus 20:8-11) God made the keeping of the Sabbath a perpetual covenant with the children of Israel. "*It is a sign between Me and the children of Israel forever; for in six days the Lord made the heavens and the earth, and on the seventh day He rested and was refreshed.*" (Exodus 31:17)

To the muslim it is unheard of that Allah would have such humanlike 'weakness,' like the need to rest and be refreshed. The South African muslim apologist Ahmed Deedat wrote in his 'Combat Kit' that the "*Sabbath is a standing insult to God in the Bible.*" He quotes Sura 2:255 as his objection to Allah being fatigued, needing a Sabbath, a rest. Jesus Christ said: "*The Sabbath was made for man, and not man for the Sabbath. Therefore the Son of Man is also Lord of the Sabbath.*" (Mark 2: 27,28) The point here, in the framework of this book, is that also here it is clear that Allah and God are not one and the same but totally different.

Note: Deedat wants muslims to purchase a Bible and to paste his 'Combat Kit' in their own copy of the Bible and use Deedat's Combat Kit "*to convert the Christian scud into a patriot missile.*" I wonder what Deedat considers the Christian 'scud.' The Bible? No Christian minister, no Chistian missionary, no Christian has the kind of attitude, or the kind of approach in their dealings with muslims that Deedat displays towards Christians! Clearly Deedat is on the war-path arousing hatred in fellow muslims and inciting them to join him in his war against Christianity! Deedat's approach to the Bible is far different from his approach towards the Koran. Such an approach to the Bible will cause the Bible never to be of any profit to Deedat nor to anyone with like mind. It is very sad to have in one's possession the means to salvation and to all that God has and is, yet because of unbelief- in Deedat's case even worse- never to profit from it. Jesus could in His own city of birth, Nazareth, do very few signs and miracles, because of the people's unbelief, especially of the religious people! (Matthew 13: 58; Mark 6: 5,6)

Chapter Thirteen

Conclusion

That Allah is nót one and the same as God, but the ancient Arabic idol of Mecca, has been overwhelmingly established here. And since Allah is nót the same as God, the translation of Allah with "God" in the media etc. is wrong; it is an abomination and a blasphemy!

I wrote the translators of the media motivated letters, requesting them not to translate Allah with God, but to leave it as Allah. My own name remains the same in any language; it is not translated. So why translate Allah? Dr. Leemhuis, the maker of a new translation of the Koran in Dutch, writes that this is done to "make the distance between us and muslims not needlessly larger than it already is." But because this is not a linguistic but a theological argument and motivation, the translator steps way out of his area of authority. He does so by deliberate choice and deliberate intention to teach the readers of his Koran-translation in Dutch that Allah and God are the same, though this is not so! But to bring muslims and 'us' closer together, Dr. Leemhuis considers the introduction of this abominable error in his translation permitted. But it is nót permitted; in fact it is Islamic dictatorship, because Dr. Leemhuis decides for the reader, and denies the reader the freedom to decide for himself and to make up his own mind for himself!

The readers, especially the nominal so called 'christians' involved in a so called 'dialogue' with muslims, need to realize that Mohammed derived many of his verses from Biblical accounts he had heard in an often distorted way and/or coloured by the theology of the people who told him. Because there existed in the time of Mohammed christian sects in the Arabic Peninsula who denied the divinity of Christ, His Sonship of God, and His crucifixion. Their view certainly fitted Mohammed's rejection of polytheism, and was either the main reason of Mohammed's rejection of polytheism and of Jesus Christ's divinity and His Sonship of God, or has at least contributed to it.

In the early days of Christianity there was much discussion, dissension, discord and controversy about the nature of Christ, involving the highest level of political and church government. This resulted even in the ex-communication of certain groups of Christianity which were marked as sects.

There was, for example, the sect of Docetism, who believed the assertion that Christ's human body was a phantasm, and that his sufferings and death were mere appearance. 'If he suffered he was not God; if he was God he did not suffer,' they taught.

There also was the sect of Gnosticism, which attempted to interpret Christ in terms of heathen philosophy, or 'theosophy.' Four types of Gnosticism have been identified, 'The Syrian Type,' "The Egyptian Type,' 'The Judaizing Type,' 'The Pontic Type.' In the framework of Islam I only want to quote here a portion of a document of a representative of the Egyptian type, Basilides, of around 130 A.D. which was reproduced in a more poetical and popular form by Valentinus, around 140 A.D.: "And he (Jesus) appeared to the nations of them as a man on the earth, and performed deeds of virtue. Wherefore he suffered not, but a certain Simon, a Cyrenian, was impressed to bear his cross for him; and Simon was crucified in ignorance and error, having been transfigured by him, that men should suppose him to be Jesus, while Jesus himself took on the appearance of Simon and stood by and mocked them..." ("Documents of the Christian Church, Selected and Edited by Henry Bettenson. Oxford University Press.) The Koran says about the same as this heretic (Sura 4: 157 D) Is the doctrine of this 'christian' sect therefore not the source of the same teaching in the Koran?

Another Christian sect was Arianism. Arius, bishop of Nicomedia, around 321 A.D., wrote "...before he was begotten or created or appointed or established, he did not exist; for he was not unbegotten. We are persecuted ('unjustly persecuted by pope Alexander,' he wrote) because we say that the Son has a beginning, but God is without beginning. For that reason we are persecuted, and because we say that he is from what is not. And this we say because he is neither part of God not derived from any substance. For this we are persecuted."

Nestorius, patriarch of Constantinople, 428-431 A.D. who did not believe that Jesus Christ is God, was condemned as a heretic at the great council of Chalcedon. Nestorianism soon found its its center in the Syrian school at Nisibis, from where it spread to Persia, and then across Asia into China and India.The Nestorian community had a continuous presence in the mountains of Kurdistan until their calamitous sufferings in the First World War after which many of the survivors moved to San Francisco.

Because the Bible was not readily available in Mohammed's time, as the printing press had not yet been invented, and the Christians themselves had no way of being corrected in their doctrines by the Bible, the Word of God, it is no wonder that so many un-Biblical doctrines of 'christian' sects could exist for so long, and travel so wide; and that so many accounts from the Bible were so distorted. And these were the things Mohammed heard. It is unlikely that Mohammed ever saw a Bible. Let alone read it, or hear it read to him. The accusation in the Koran that Christians and Jews have tampered with the Scriptures is therefore not based on facts, but on their rejection of Mohammed.

Not only were the accounts of the Bible that Mohammed adopted in the Koran distorted by the sectarian sources he derived them from, in the Koran they are all disconnected from the connection in which they are found in the Bible where they all find their centre in, and point to Christ. *"Not unjustly Mohammed announced what he said as being something new, for also that much he derived from the Bible, received a new centre, which is found in the peculiar revelation view that Mohammed offered, which turned out to make himself the centre, where only that which he conveyed could be accepted as authoritative. Through this everything changed colour, has a new structure, a new construction from a new central thought. Because of this not a single concept from the Koran can be equalized with a corresponding Biblical given, however much they may look alike. When the Koran talks about the covenant of Allah, through it's structure is different from when the Bible mentions the covenant of God, and the holiness that the Koran mentions is different from the holiness of the Bible, and the Isa (Jesus) of the Koran is another than the Jesus of the Gospel, and the Abraham of the Koran is different than the one of* *whom the Old Testament testifies, and this same applies to all concepts and thoughts that the Bible and Koran seem to have in common; think for example of the paradise in the Koran, and the paradise in the Bible. That is why it was often wrongly thought that communication with muslims would be easy because of much that was thought to be in common, for which no discussion would be needed. This, however, time and again turned out a disappointment, for the above mentioned reason."* (Prof. Dr. D.S. Attema in "De Koran"; Kok, Kampen)

In the Koran-verses that are quoted in this book, there are often clear references to events and people in Scripture and we would therefore be easily tempted to conclude that Mohammed is speaking about God. Yet because Mohammed inserted the-god, Allah, the ancient idol of the Arabs, in the portions of Scripture adopted in the Koran, and because everything has changed colour in the Koran (see remark of Prof. Attema) we have to be continually on guard in reading verses from the Koran that it is not God that is spoken about - though it seems to be so. It seems confusing, because the false thing looks sometimes like the real thing. But this is the most effective of lies and deception of satan, as is proven by the long time it has been around.
It is a very bad development that publishers and authors of Koran versions in English, Dutch etc. have started using God for Allah, and Mary for Miriam. Such versions of the Koran, that have been adapted to accommodate for the dialogue between nominal 'christians' and muslims, and to assure the acceptance of Western university disciplines like islamologists, Arabists by an increasing amount of muslims in the West, make it much harder to discern and resist the lie, and not to fall for it.

In my quotes I have therefore replaced their false translation of Allah with God, with the original Allah. For the translation of Allah with God is grammatically incorrect. And because the arguments motivating this linguistic error are not grammatical but theological arguments. Dr. Leemhuis, the maker of a new translation of the Koran in Dutch, writes, *"The name Allah is also used by Arabic Christians for God. Therefore it deserves preference to use the name God* (is no name but a title) *instead of Allah in translations of islamic texts, not to make the distance between us and muslims needlessly larger than it is"*.

The co-worker of the newly revised Kramer Koran version in Dutch, the Arabist Dr. J.J.G. Jansen, wrote in an article responding to an earlier article by me in the Dutch newspaper "Nederlands Dagblad" that Arabic church communities for centuries have been using the word Allah for God in translations of Christian texts and of the Scriptures. *"A better (or other) argument for translating Allah with 'God', does not exist"*, he writes.

It is amazing that these scholars use such unscholarly arguments in their defence and justification of their prejudicial error. Clearly the latter argument could also have been used decades ago but this did not lead the translators then to translate Allah with God; they simply left it. (At that time there was no 'dialogue' with muslims.) These modern translators, though accusing me of not respecting the tradition of the Arabic Christian communities who have been using Allah for God for centuries, themselves do not follow the tradition of their predecessors whose translation they have revised. Not only thát, but I dó respect the tradition of Arab Christians, but nót the tradition that developed after their islamic occupation and domination, which adopted the error of their islamic occupiers, who even in the Arabic language that the Arab Christians had to use (The Arabic script was developed during those centuries) excepted only one god, the-god 'Allah.' I accept the much older tradition of the Arab Christians, of the time before islam, when the Arab Christians used the word 'Ilah' for 'God' (actually Arabic knows no capital letters, but for clarification purposes I do so here).

It may be painful for Arab Christians, and for all those other Christians in whose languages Allah has been used and is being used for God for centuries, to discontinue that, but it is better than to continue in a grave error which has weakened the faith of Arab Christians and the Arab church for so many centuries.

Chapter Fourteen

Attention

Unless explicitly told by God, for the right reasons; not just out of curiosity, be careful about possessing the Koran. Two friends of mine who are ex-muslim converts to Christ, told me they were ordered by the Lord Jesus to get rid of their Koran. They did not argue with God about that, but obeyed Him. But readers, who are unfamiliar with the tactics of satan, his operations, and with the demonic world, may argue. But spiritually discerning people know that there is a spirit behind the Koran.

There also are spirits behind the Buddah-statues, behind the Zodiac signs, behind the Ankh-crosses and the Scarabs both from ancient idolatrous Egypt, all of these nowadays so popular in the rebellious West (I already quoted 1 Samuel 15:23 that *"rebellion is as the sin of witchcraft,"* and this is a clear evidence of that) and there are spirits behind the 'hand of Fatima' very much in use in the Islamic world, and there are so many other idolatrous objects which all have spirits behind.

The word of God clearly commands us, *"Nor shall you bring an abomination into your house, lest you be doomed to destruction like it. You shall utterly detest it and utterly abhor it, for it is an accursed thing."* (Deuteronomy 7:26 NKJV)

When I purchased the Koran to be able to quote verses from it in this book, I felt that spirit. It is a pious spirit, it is a lying spirit. It seeks to slowly take hold of a person who opens up when reading the Koran.

Because all muslims have surrendered to this spirit (Islam means 'surrender.') of Islam, Allah, and are bound by it through the deception of Islam, muslims cannot logically, rationally consider the facts as presented here. But the spirit of Islam, Allah, causes muslims to respond to his exposure by the truth with violence and hatred in a very irrational, inhuman way, blinding him from the truth. It is like a reflex and the muslim may not even understand why he responds in this way.

The initial response of ex-muslim convert to Christ, bishop John A. Subhan of the Methodist Episcopal Church in Hyderabad, India, is typical of the response of most muslims . When a muslim friend had first given him a copy of the Gospel from the Bible, he had responded by tearing it to pieces! He had not even looked through it! But the truth, especially the truth about Allah and Islam, triggers the spirit of Allah in a muslim to respond with hatred and violence, like the reflex of a person who touches a hot stove.

Is therefore any hope for the muslim who wants to know the truth? Yes, there is, as I explain in the chapter on how to be saved. But it does require the muslim to wilfully and verbally renounce Allah, Islam, Mohammed and the Koran. This medicine may taste very bitter to the muslim, but it is the only medicine to life. As a spiritual doctor, this is the only remedy to life from death and deception I can offer the muslim on his way to eternal damnation, after having diagnosed the spiritual condition of the muslim by means of the truth. This renouncing should not be done without God's protection and covering, which is given by accepting the true God and Jesus Christ. This covering is given by spiritual implication and application of the blood of Jesus Christ. The muslim may simply say, "Jesus Christ, if You are the Truth, and the Life and the only way to God, cover me with Your blood! Protect me!" The muslim should then further pray the prayer I have written at the end of my explanation on how to be saved.

It is an evil thing that in the West nowadays university students in disciplines to become Arabists, etc. are told from the start to open up (to the spirit of islam), and to let go of their barriers, and of their logic, etc. though of course not in such words. By doing so they open up to be demonised, and clearly this is the case with all or virtually all of the ones taught in such disciplines. (* 1)

Yet these are the ones hired as so called experts, to give their comments about Islam in the Western media, newspapers, etc. when they can only do so outwardly, never substantially, spiritually. And the Western media, publishers and the like rather publish comments, articles, books etc. by such demonised or at least demonically influenced students and graduates, than by those like me who know God and who discern the spirit of islam. Thus they ask council from those who are deceived and inevitably influenced by the spirit of Islam in the study of their discipline, and do not discern the spirit of Islam, and reject the spiritual counsel of servants of God. Only because the university world gave them titles and such. But how else can islam be judged except spiritually? But since the Western media reject spiritual things, they can only deal with the matter of Islam outwardly, never substantially! That is why they are instruments that deceive many! Jesus Christ speaks about "*blind leaders of the blind. And if the blind leads the blind, both will fall into the ditch.*" (Matthew 15: 14; Luke 6:39)

And even many, if not most, Christians working amongst muslims are often very much tainted and influenced by the spirit of islam. There are even Spirit-filled Christian ministers who say: "*Allah to be essentially the same as Jehovah*"- a quote from "The New Millennium" from Dr. Pat Robertson, president of CBN (* 2), who even writes that Mohammed is a prophet of God, etc. (I repeatedly wrote Dr. Pat Robertson about it, asking him to correct this error publicly, but he never even acknowledged receiving my letter. Nowadays – thank God!- he has changed his tune, and view!)

Such a division and weakness within the 'christian' camp against the fundamentally anti-christian (enemy of) islam is one of the reasons islam is advancing in such a way in the West. (Islamic war is also won in bed; for muslim families are large, while Western families who selfishly pursue materialism and hedonism are of limited size) by their deliberate choice. Worse yet, it keeps muslims in their state of eternal damnation! It is disobedience to Jesus Christ!

The statement you hear muslims make that "Islam is the fastest growing religion in the world" is denied by the statistics! The only method by which islam from the beginning has grown was by the sword! Nowadays the only growth is in births to muslim-parents, but hardly by any conversions. And 75% of those who 'convert' to islam, revert to their former state within a couple of years!

Warning: Translations of this book, or of portions of it, into Arabic or into other languages who have been using the word 'Allah' for 'God', should no longer use Allah for God, but Ilah! I urge this also for Bible versions and all other Christian books etc. in these

languages. In the same way the quotes of verses of the Koran in translations of this book should not use the word God for Allah, but leave it as Allah. I have done so here myself. I also refused to copy the word Mary that the modern translators have begun to use in their new versions and revisions of the Koran. Because the Koran does not use the name Mary, but the name Miriam, the name of the sister of Moses and Aaron. Koran translators should stick with their task of correctly translating the text, not try to improve on it by adapting it because of theological or other reasons!

* Note 1: Occultists, hypnotists etc. require the same thing; they open up and ask the people to open up to what they call 'energies.' Since these energies are spiritual (as they cannot be measured physiologically) they can never be of God, who is one of the two spiritual sources in the universe. Because God does not work through people who are not His, they are of satan, the second spiritual source in the universe. Whenever I read or hear people speak about 'energies,' I know they speak of demons, though they are the first to deny it! No wonder, they are deceived by the very demons operating through them.

* Note 2: CBN stands for Christian Broadcasting Network. It is one of the major Christian television- and radio-networks in the USA, broadcasting it's anchor-show, "The 700 Club," from coast to coast every day. It also operates internationally. The tremendous testimony of how Pat Robertson was born-again, and founded CBN, starting with one little TV-station in Portsmouth, Virginia, can be read in the book "Shout it from the housetops." I translated this book into Dutch. This book is a tremendous testimony of how God can take a man who knew absolutely nothing of television, and use him in it. It is a tremendous testimony of how God can use television and radio to save people, to heal people emotionally inwardly and outwardly of all kinds of diseases and problems, and to touch people in many other ways.. God does that every day in the USA through CBN's '700-Club.' But in the area of Islam, Pat Robertson apparently went out of his area of anointing. Without checking the information he has probably simply copied the information given him by someone he respected and trusted; someone he thought knew Islam. Alas, through his book, Pat Robertson has falsely informed his readers, who in turn trusted him.

Chapter Fifteen

The Gospel of Jesus Christ unto salvation of all who appropriate it into their lives

I would like to share with you the good news of the gospel of Jesus Christ. Many people have either never heard the gospel, or they may have heard and even believe the facts about the gospel but have never appropriated the gospel into their own lives, making their belief of none effect. They usually don't know how to appropriate it into their lives, nor that it needs to be appropriated before it leads to their salvation.

It is of the utmost importance that everybody considers God, and the reasons for his or her existence, preferably as early in life as possible. Does God exist? The Bible says: "*The fool has said in his heart, 'There is no God.'*" (Psalm 14:1)

The existence of God can even be seen by use of logic. For, suppose someone is in a desert or on planet Mars, Jupiter or whatever. And suppose he sees a craft, like a plane, a vehicle, a spacecraft. By simply looking at them, one can already know that there is someone who made these. And that that someone has intelligence, and knows the laws of gravity, of friction, of thermodynamics etc., and has applied these laws to make his creation. One can know that the creator has power. For he obviously has the ability to find ore and then to subtract the metals from the ore and then to shape these into the desired product. Etc. Therefore a person who lives on planet earth, can, by looking at the planet, know that there is a creator, who must be greater than any person on earth, to create even mankind, and to cause the laws into operation that make this planet and the universe and everything in it run organised and not haphazardly.

God says in the book of Romans in the Bible, that "*since the creation of the world His invisible attributes are clearly seen, being understood by the things that are made, even His eternal power and Godhead.*" (Romans 1: 20 NKJV) So, by use of logic applied to understand the things that are made, man can clearly see that there is a powerful God, that He is eternal, that He is organised, and further attributes of Him.

It is sad that most people nowadays suppress the truth by their sin and unrighteousness, as we can see all around us, which shows the reality of the Word of God, Romans 1: 18 - 32, which says:

"For the wrath of God is revealed from heaven against all ungodliness and unrighteousness of men, who hold the truth in unrighteousness; Because that which may be known of God is manifest in them; for God hath showed it unto them. For the invisible things of him from the creation of the world are clearly seen, being understood by the things that are made, even his eternal power and Godhead; so that they are without excuse: Because that, when they knew God, they glorified him not as God, neither were thankful; but became vain in their imaginations, and their foolish heart was darkened. Professing themselves to be wise, they became fools, And changed the glory of the incorruptible God into an image made like to corruptible man, and to birds, and four-footed beasts, and creeping things. Wherefore God also gave them up to uncleanness through the lusts of their own hearts, to dishonour their own bodies between themselves: Who changed the truth of God into a lie, and worshipped and served the creature more than the Creator, who is blessed for ever. Amen. ✷

For this cause God gave them up unto vile affections: for even their women did change the natural use into that which is against nature: And likewise also the men, leaving the natural use of the woman, burned in their lust one toward another; men with men working that which is unseemly, and receiving in themselves that recompense of their error which was meet. And even as they did not like to retain God in their knowledge, God gave them over to a reprobate mind, to do those things which are not convenient;

Being filled with all unrighteousness, fornication, wickedness, covetousness, maliciousness; full of envy, murder, debate, deceit, malignity; whisperers, Backbiters, haters of God, despiteful, proud, boasters, inventors of evil things, disobedient to parents, 31 Without understanding, covenant-breakers, without natural affection, implacable, unmerciful: Who knowing the judgment of God, that they which commit such things are worthy of death, not only do the same, but have pleasure in them that do them."

 Knowing that there is a God does not give a person the ability to know God. Knowing about Him is vastly different from knowing Him. I'll explain that unless God reveals Himself to us, no man can know Him, no matter how he tries.

Before you go any further, it is imperative that you now realise and know in your heart, that there is a God, Who created the universe with a design and plan. And that you want to know God, and your place, your purpose in His plan; and how you and God relate, beyond just as Creator and creature. Unless you first realise that there is a God, it is of no use to find out Who He is and how to relate to Him.

God revealed Himself to man from the very beginning He created him. After all His whole purpose for creating mankind was to have a partner in His own image, that He could relate and fellowship with. After man sinned, God's communication with man was cut of, except for certain instances and certain people He chose to communicate with to accomplish His purposes. Sin always cuts of communication and relationship with God; this is called spiritual death. But in order to communicate and relate with God, man needs to have the very nature of God. Because God is spirit, and man is flesh, man has to also be born of the Spirit in order to become a spiritual being as well. This is why Jesus Christ said, "*Most assuredly, I say to you, unless one is born again, he cannot see the kingdom of God." "Most assuredly, I say to you, unless one is born of water and the Spirit, he cannot enter the kingdom of God. That which is born of the flesh is flesh, and that which is born of the Spirit is spirit."* (John 3:3,5,6)

The way to be born of God is by repenting of one's own ways, by believing, receiving and appropriating by faith Jesus' accomplished work at the cross of Calvary, Who shed His blood, died our death, underwent the penalty for our sins. "*But as many as received Him, to them He gave the right to become children of God, to those who believe in His name: who were born, not of blood, nor of the will of the flesh, nor of the will of man, but of God."* (John 1:12,13) To even be able to begin to communicate with God, or for God to communicate with us, we need to have the same nature as God (2 Peter 1: 3,4), and be spiritually alive. We cannot even receive, let alone understand, God's written communication, that He inspired the authors of the Bible, God's Word, to write down, unless we have been born again. It is utter folly, visible in religious circles all around, to try to understand that which is of the Spirit with the human mind. (1 Corinthians 2: 13,14)

How do we know this all to be true? For one, God says so, and I have, together with countless millions throughout these past 2000 years, personally experienced being born again, as a result of acting upon Gods Word.

But there are those who will object:: *"Isn't the Bible written by human beings, and can it therefore be called the Word of God, and can it be trusted as such; more so, does it have the authority of God?"*

Let me illustrate. If my mother sent out my younger brother with the message that I had to do a certain thing, and my younger brother told me exactly as my mother related to him, I had better do what he related to me as the message of my mother to me. If I did not do it, saying something like, well, 'my brother is playing a joke with me', or 'my mother didn't tell that to him,' while my mother did send him, and he related the message correctly, I suffered the consequences!
God being Spirit related His Word through the individuals He chose. Think about it: How else could God, being Spirit, relate His Word, His communication into the natural realm but through those who are of the natural realm? They did not write presumptuously out of their own initiative. (2 Peter 1:21; 2 Timothy 3:16,17)

It is beyond the scope of this treatise to further establish the fact that the Bible is God's Word. The reader who experiences the witness in his heart that what is written here is truth and acts upon it, he/she will experience the new birth of the Spirit of God and become a new creation. (2 Corinthians 5:17)

But if the reader argues within him - or herself, saying, 'These are the author's own words, and also the Bible is written by men, and does not obey what God says through us, he or she will suffer the consequences;

the ultimate consequence is to end up in the lake that burns with fire and brimstone for all eternity! (Revelation 21:8) For if we do not believe God's Word through His messengers, we will suffer the consequences from God Himself!

God being Spirit had to communicate through chosen human vessels so His communication could be heard in the natural realm. Now that God in these last days makes His Spirit available to all who have been born again, He can again communicate directly to all who have His Spirit. But God never communicates anything that is in conflict with His written Word, the canonical Bible. Anything and everything that conflicts with the Bible, rightly divided as the Spirit teaches, has to be rejected as error. (**For this very reason the Koran has to be rejected!** And even the Apocryphical books, cannot be accepted as the canonical Word of God!)

Therefore it is imperative in these last days to know the Word of God, the Bible, rightly divided, so we will not be deceived by all kinds of false doctrine, and go off to a way which seems right, but which leads unto death. (Proverbs 14:12; 16:25)

To measure, one needs the right measuring rod. That is why such care has been taken to establish a standard meter!

Nowadays we are ruled by fools, for they reject God, who have made themselves the measuring rod. No wonder the peoples of the nations suffer! For fools do not know how to make just laws!

Why is Jesus Christ the only way to God? Why can we only be saved through Jesus Christ?

First, because God says so in His Word. Jesus said, "*I am the way, the truth, and the life. No one comes to the Father except through Me.*" (John 14:6) "*Nor is there salvation in any other, for there is no other name under heaven given among men by which we must be saved.*" (Acts 4:12)

The second reason is because only Jesus Christ paid the penalty for our sins for us, by dying at the cross, "*For Christ also suffered once* *for sins, the just* (Christ) *for the unjust* (we)*, that He might bring us to God, being put to death in the flesh but made alive by the Spirit* (2 Peter 3:18)

Jesus Christ is the only one so far, who rose again from the dead without ever dying again, declaring by His resurrection from the dead that He is the Son of God(Romans 1:4 "*...and by Him* (Jesus Christ) *to reconcile all things to Himself* (the Father)*...having made peace through the blood of His cross...now He has reconciled in the body of His flesh through death.*" (Colossians 1:20-22)

Let me illustrate. Assuming you trespass the law, say you drove through a red traffic light. You are caught and stand before the judge. He asks if you are guilty, and you, being honest, besides it's on the photo, acknowledge you did it and thus are found guilty. The judge then says he will have to satisfy the requirement of the law, which says that the penalty of trespassing the law is payment of a certain amount, or prison, or both. Without a penalty for trespassing the law, a law is powerless, and really no law at all. Also, the judge cannot let it go by unpunished, because then he would not be a just judge. For whom will he let go free, and on what basis, and whom will he punish?

So, if the judge does not fulfil the requirement of the law, by punishing the trespasser, he does injustice, and makes himself an unjust judge. So, the judge fines you a certain amount to pay for trespassing the law that says that it is forbidden to drive through a red traffic-light. Now, suppose you don't have the money to pay your fine; that would mean certain prison term to satisfy the law. But suppose someone else, a friend, has the money, and offers it to you, because he wants to save you from prison. You then have two options. One, you refuse, because you don't want to be in debt to the other; or you want to remain independent, and you don't even want to be grateful to someone else for doing something you could not do; your pride cannot accept that.

The other option is that you accept. You then give the money to the judge, and he will accept that money, and not say, 'Well, this is not your money, it was given to you, I cannot accept it.' No, he will accept it, and you are free, the demand of the law has been satisfied, and you can never again be prosecuted for this offence.

95

The fact is that before God we are all guilty of sin. (Romans 3:23; 1 John 1:8) And the wages of sin is death. Spiritual death in this life (Ephesians 2:1-7), and eternal death, the second death, separated from God for ever, yet alive to suffer eternally in the lake that burns with fire and brimstone. (Revelation 21:8)

If we had to pay the penalty for our own sins, we would be eternally lost, and all go into the lake of fire and brimstone. But God loved us so much that He gave His only begotten Son, Who paid the penalty for our sins by dying at the cross in our place. He died our death! He suffered our death-penalty. In this way He showed His great love for us, as well as opened the way for us to be free from the penalty of our sins and trespasses, so that we can be reconciled to God and live with Him for ever! We are also freed from the consequences of sins in general, like curses, death, sickness, diseases. And we are freed from the power of sin!

But though Jesus Christ paid the penalty for our sins, we have two options open to us. One, we reject Jesus Christ's offer of paying the penalty for our sins, and pridefully, independently, choose to pay the penalty, the consequences of our sins ourselves: suffering in the lake of fire and brimstone for ever. Or you accept Jesus Christ's offer of paying the penalty for your sin. This is God's desire for you.

Most people who have been raised in a nominal 'Christian' family, who have been going to church for the greatest part of their youth or life, know the *facts about* Jesus Christ's birth from the virgin Mary, His life, His ministry, His walk with His disciples, His teachings, His working of miracles and healings, casting out of demons, His conflicts with the Jewish religious leaders of that time, His suffering, His death at the cross of Calvary, His resurrection from the dead on the third day, His ascension to heaven in His resurrected body in which He appeared to His disciples for 40 days after His resurrection, and the many prophecies concerning the Messiah He fulfilled even in the smallest details. These are historical facts which have been recorded not only by the New Testament authors but also by Roman and Jewish historians, and if anyone disputes these facts, he cannot believe any historical fact about any person or any event in all of history! (These historians say nothing of the spiritual implications of the historical facts about Jesus Christ; their accounts simply give more credence to the historic authenticity and accuracy of the accounts and of the Bible.)

Though these people have been outwardly raised as Christians, their mental acceptance of the historical facts about Jesus Christ has not led to their salvation, to their being born of God.

Let me explain this with another illustration. A person may know all the facts there are to know about a bridge. However, unless he gives his life over to the bridge and starts walking across the bridge, following the road of the bridge, he will never reach the other side. That bridge might as well have never been built for that person. Though he knows all the facts about the bridge, he acts as an unbeliever, who does not believe that he can reach the other side through that bridge. But a simple person who knows nothing about the bridge but that the bridge can take him to the other side, who shows his faith in that simple fact by trusting his life to the bridge and walks across the bridge to the other side, is the one who profits of the bridge; not the one who knows all the facts about it, but who never acts out that faith. Most people view the person who knows the facts about the bridge as a believer, but that is not the Biblical view. The Biblical view is that a believer is someone who acts out his belief; faith without works, the required action, is dead (James 2:14-26).

Jesus Christ is **the** Bridge to God. There is no other one Those who have been raised in the church mentally agree with, and 'believe' the facts about the bridge with their minds, but they have never given their lives over to the bridge, Jesus Christ. Therefore the Bridge, Jesus Christ profits them nothing! They end up in the lake of fire and brimstone like all unbelievers. (Rev. 21:8)

For the unbeliever on this earth, it is easier to be saved than these. Because the nominal Christian lives in the delusion that he is fine because he knows something about Jesus Christ. The unbeliever is more willing to listen to these instructions and information than these. Therefore the unbeliever is more likely to give his life to Jesus Christ and be saved, than these. And these nominal 'christians' will end up like any unbeliever if they don't give their lives over to the Bridge, and make their mental knowledge of the facts about Jesus Christ, experiential knowledge. Because of their beliefs it is much more difficult for muslims, Buddist, Hindus, Mormons, Yehovah Witnesses, etc. to accept the truth of the Gospel of Jesus Christ, and to give their lives to Him, and be saved. Because they are all under the delusion that they are safe and okay in their belief and way!

Now, whether you were raised with the facts about Jesus Christ or not, you can now be born again; as Scripture sais: "*Behold, now is the accepted time; behold, now is the day of salvation*" (2 Corinthians 6:2); you can now experience being brought to God, through the only Bridge to God, the only way to God: Jesus Christ. As this is a spiritual birth, it takes a spiritual action to experience it: prayer, repentance, belief in action, acceptance with the heart, trust in God.

So if you will pray this prayer, not just with your mind but with your heart, meaning and believing it, expecting Jesus Christ to make you a child of God, it will be done.

Lord Jesus Christ, I ask YOU to bind all demons from manifesting in me and from trying to prevent me from praying this prayer, and from hurting me and from even trying to kill me. Send Your angels to help me.

Acts 2: 38 & 39 says:
"*Repent, and be baptized every one of you in the name of Jesus Christ for the remission of sins, and ye shall receive the gift of the Holy Ghost. For the promise is unto you, and to your children, and to all that are afar off, even as many as the LORD our God shall call.*" He ís calling you now, and as your respond, and become His child, you KNÓW, He called you. Otherwise you would not be reading this!

Pray: Lord Jesus Christ, I come to you, right now, and I acknowledge that I am a sinner in need of You. (Romans 3:23; Luke 18:13) I come to You by faith in Your Word. I believe that You took on the form of a man so You could die, as God cannot die, humbling Yourself to be a servant, obedient even unto death. (John 3:16; mark 16:16-18) I believe You lived a perfect life without committing any sin, so YOU could be a perfect sacrifice, and so that YOU could take my sins upon YOU and be killed for my sins, in my place, instead of me. I believe YOU died for my sins at the cross at Calvary. I believe You rose from the dead on the third day, and after 40 days ascended unto heaven from where You will return to judge and reign.

Lord Jesus Christ, Heavenly father, God, I repent (Luke 3:13; Acts 3:19). I repent from going my own way; from doing my own thing, from thinking my own thoughts, from doing things against YOUR will. I repent from every sin in my life. I turn around; I repent: I turn my back on those things, on those thoughts and on those actions and on those attitudes which are NOT according to YOUR WILL. I turn AWAY FROM my sins, and towards YOU, Lord Jesus Christ COMPLETELY, for YOU are the ONLY begotten Son of God, and THE ONLY WAY to Father God (not just one of many ways; YOU are the ONLY WAY to God, for ONLY YOU gave YOUR life for me, at the cross at Calvary! I forsake my own, wicked way and my own wicked thoughts, and turn to You, Lord Jesus Christ! (Isaiah 55:7)

I surrender myself to You, Lord Jesus Christ. As You already paid the penalty for my sins, I accept Your death for me. I accept You, Lord Jesus Christ, as my personal Saviour. Lord Jesus Christ, forgive my sins (*1), and cleanse me from all unrighteousness with the blood of Jesus Christ. (*2) (1 John 1:9) I surrender the Lordship of my life over to YOU. You paid for my life, by YOUR precious blood. I am YOUR legal property now, Lord Jesus Christ! Therefore, not only be My Saviour but also be MY LORD; MY KING and reign in and over me! (John 1:11-13; Revelation 3:20) I give You control over my life Lord Jesus Christ! I open the door of my heart and ask You, Lord Jesus Christ: Come into My life, and live Your life in me.

Lord Jesus Christ, HELP ME, RECEIVE ME, TAKE MY HAND and never let me go! As You already paid the penalty for my sins, I accept Your death for me, and receive from You Your LIFE and ETERNAL LIFE in exchange for my death, and the freedom from the consequences of my sins and the freedom from the power of sin to live a life pleasing unto YOU, into my life. Lord Jesus Christ, come into my life! I receive spiritual life from You even unto eternity, because YOU the eternal ONE came into me by Your Spirit.

I renounce all other gods. I renounce all that is not of You, Lord Jesus Christ. I renounce all agreements with satan.

For the muslim: I renounce Allah, Islam, Mohammed and the Koran, so I may be able to receive the true God and the true Jesus Christ, God's Son; His Truth, His life, His will, His love, His forgiveness, His peace, and His purpose in my life, and the adoption as a child of God, in Jesus' name. I accept the covenant of God dedicated with the blood of Jesus. I seal my renunciation and prayer and commitment with the blood of Jesus, in Jesus' name.

For the Mormon: I renounce the false god Mormonism teaches. I renounce the book of Mormon and the other books of Mormonism. I renounce all the rituals of Mormonism, and every dedication I made to Mormonism, so I can receive the true God, and the truth of God and Jesus Christ, and new life in Him, etcetera. (see above)

The Yehovah witness, the Buddist, the Hindu, the Freemason, etcetera can verbally speak out similar renounciations as applicable to their specific situation.

I ask You now, heavenly Father to make me Your child, right now. Let me be born of God right now. Make me a new creation in Christ Jesus, right now. I open the door of my heart, Lord Jesus, and I ask You to come into my heart, and live Your life in me, from this day forth, by Your Spirit. (Revelation 3:20)

Drive out from me, from my body, the temple of Your Holy Spirit, all that is not of You, Lord Jesus Christ, as You drove out the money changers, the buyers and sellers from the temple in Jerusalem (John 2:13-22)

Help me and guide me to clean up my life, and to drive out the 'ites' from my promised land. Deliver me from all demons, from all curses, from all demonic activity, Lord Jesus Christ. Heavenly Father, give me Your Holy Spirit. Lord Jesus, baptize me with Your Holy Spirit. (*3)

Dear Jesus, teach me Your Word. Place me into Your Body of believers. (Ephesians 4:11-16; Matthew 18:15-20; 28:18-20; Mark 16:16-18; 1 Corinthians 12,13,14; Hebrews 10:24,25 Etc.)

Thank You, heavenly Father, for accepting me, in Jesus Christ, and for making me Your child this moment, in Jesus Name, AMEN!

Thank You, Lord, for hearing and answering my prayer!

Now tell others that Jesus Christ saved you. Because God says in His Word: "*that if you confess with your mouth the Lord Jesus and believe in your heart that God has raised Him from the dead, you will be saved. For with the heart one believes unto righteousness, and with the mouth confession is made unto salvation.*" (Romans 10:9,10)

God bless you as you do this. Now continue:

I ask You Holy Spirit, Lord Jesus Christ, to show me every sin You want me to confess and turn away from - take your time for that; make a list of it, if this helps, and cross off every sin He has brought into your remembrance that you have confessed and received His forgiveness and cleansing for with His blood.

But be aware of the accusations of our enemy, satan! The Holy Spirit convicts of sin; but satan accuses. When satan accuses you, there is always unrest in your soul, an unsettledness, an uncertainty, a false guilt. And satan continues to bring accusation against you, so there is a battle, until satan sees that you have learned to discern his accusations, and to cast them aside, as YOU MUST BELIEVE THAT JESUS CHRIST HAS FORGIVEN YOU, AFTER YOU HAVE CONFESSED YOUR SINS AND TURNED AWAY FROM THEM!, paying no longer any attention to satan's accusation, and to the nagging feeling in you; you MUST accept God's forgiveness by faith; just as you must receive anything and everything you ask for, and by His Word says he has given you, BY FAITH believing and trusting Him! The unrest in your soul; this unsettled feeling of guilt is not so when the Holy Spirit convicts you of sin, then there is a certainty and a peace about it, when He speaks to your heart.

I ask You Father God, to forgive me my sins and to cleanse me from all unrighteousness with the blood of Jesus Christ (this is spiritual). (1John 1:9)

You must also forgive yourself, which is: when you trust God has forgiven you, you should not hold yourself guilty any longer either, but appropriate His forgiveness! Many people who accept satan's accusations and feel guilty, and therefore feel they deserve punishment from God...but as He no longer remembers the sins we have confessed, and therefore does not punish us, as His Son, Jesus Christ was already punished for our sins, *resolve their FALSE feelings of guilt by.... punishing themselves!* This is wrong, for this would make you judge, instead of Him.

Many religious people who really want to please God, fall into this trap of satan! For satan wants to rob our joy. Satan wants to rob our peace! Satan keeps reminding me what we have done bad and that we deserve punishment!

But since God no longer holds us guilty after we confess our sins, but declares us the righteousness of God in Christ Jesus and remembers our sins no more, we should resist satan's lies and accusations with the Word of God, declaring: "Get behind me, satan for Jesus Christ has forgiven my sins, who are you to remind me of these sins, which have been done away with?

Now, you cán employ satan by saying: "Satan that's old stuff, which Jesus Christ has already forgiven me. When satan accuses you of something, tell him: "Thank you, satan for telling me...is there anything you see I have not yet confessed to God? Tell me! I will be so grateful if you tell me more so I can repent of this also and get closer to God as I ask His forgiveness and cleansing with His blood!"

Now! You MUST also forgive everyone for what théy may have done against you! For if you do not forgive every one what they have done against you, God cannot forgive you, and then you cannot receive His life, nor anything else from Him! No blessing, no healing, no deliverance, no blessing, nothing! UNTIL you forgive from your heart everyone. Now, this MAY be difficult, but you HAVE to CHOOSE to forgive! It's a choice, not feelings; if you have problems doing it from the heart, ask God to help you.

Say: Lord Jesus Christ, heavenly Father, I find it difficult to forgive (name the person). But because I trust YOU and because You command us to forgive others, I CHOOSE to FORGIVE (name that person again). Help me, Father God, to do it from my heart, completely! I release that person into my forgiveness!

Now every time afterward that that person's thoughts still bring anger or other emotional reaction; simply bring it back to God and say: I have forgiven this person; Father God, this person is in Your hands. I refuse to be bothered by any sinful anger or other emotion or feeling, or any other sinful reaction in me the thoughts of this person causes in me!

Usually it will greatly help to start praying on behalf of, for, that person. Ask God to show you how to pray for him/ her/ them. You will see how your attitude changes as you do this!

Also, if you have stolen anything, you MUST give it back! If you have done anything wrong against anyone; you must not only ask the Lord God to forgive you, but also must you go to that person and ask him or her or them to forgive you! (this may take some time to do, so just continue this prayer, but afterward, make a list of these persons) You MUST AMMEND anything you have done wrong to anyone.

* Note 1: name every specific sin that the Holy Spirit brings into your mind; take your time for that; but be aware of the accusations of our enemy, satan. The Holy Spirit convicts of sin; but satan accuses. When satan accuses you, there is always unrest in your soul, an unsettledness, an uncertainty. And satan continues to bring accusation against you, so there is a battle, until satan sees that you have learned to discern his accusations, and to cast them aside, paying no longer any attention to it. This is not so when the Holy Spirit convicts you of sin, then there is a certainty about it.. After you have confessed your sin, and asked and accepted God's forgiveness, do not allow satan to accuse you of it; or yourself to pick it back up; God has forgiven it; He remembers it no

more. So, do likewise. Otherwise, when you pick it back up, or feel bad over it again when satan accuses you, you display unbelief towards God; because then you do not believe that He has really forgiven you, when He says in His Word He forgives you!

* Note 2: This is a spiritual application of that which Jesus' shedding of blood in the natural accomplished in every realm.

* Note 3: These areas may need the ministry of more mature fellow believers, or ministers of Jesus Christ, to be fully accomplished. But I did not want to leave them out from being asked from God already. Because these areas are of major importance to the Christian life, and sadly enough not ministered, nor even taught in many Christian churches.

Finally, our **Iniquities** need to be dealt with in our lives! When sin is forgiven and cleansed by the Blood of Jesus Christ, it is gone. But the 'programming' that makes us want to do that sin again and again, which is called INIQUITY, is still in our lives, until we have reprogrammed our lives! Because most churches do not do this; they do not even teach this so vitally important area, many churches do not manifest the true Christ, in the way He desires to manifest. Many people in the church therefore are sick, many are poor, many are defeated, discouraged, and just do not live the victorious and abundant LIFE Jesus Christ promised His children! (John 10) There are a few books out that give more insight now. Look for them and ask the Lord to teach you, and He will guide you to find the right books.

Then dó get some wine and bread to have communion; if not, get it after the prayer or at the earliest occasion - YOU make the occasion! (you see later what for); in USA etc. grape-juice is often preferred in Charismatic-, evangelical- or other protestant- churches, but I, personally think that when Scripture mentions 'wine', it's real 'wine,' not grape-juice, for when apostle Paul addresses some irregularities during the communion in the church in Corinth, he says some people were getting drunk, (1 Cor.11:21) and no one gets drunk from grape-juice. But possibly grape-juice will do. Follow your own conscience after you submit our conscience to the Lord Jesus Christ. Read the portion of

Scripture about the communion, and have communion, alone, if necessary! It is good and Biblical to have communion every day!

"Verily, verily, I say unto you, He that believeth on me hath everlasting life. I am that bread of life. Your fathers did eat manna in the wilderness, and are dead. This is the bread which cometh down from heaven, that a man may eat thereof, and not die. I am the living bread which came down from heaven: if any man eat of this bread, he shall live for ever: and the bread that I will give is my flesh, which I will give for the life of the world. The Jews therefore strove among themselves, saying, How can this man give us his flesh to eat? Then Jesus said unto them, Verily, verily, I say unto you, Except ye eat the flesh of the Son of man, and drink his blood, ye have no life in you. Whoso eateth my flesh, and drinketh my blood, hath eternal life; and I will raise him up at the last day. For my flesh is meat indeed, and my blood is drink indeed. He that eateth my flesh, and drinketh my blood, dwelleth in me, and I in him. As the living Father hath sent me, and I live by the Father: so he that eateth me, even he shall live by me. This is that bread which came down from heaven: not as your fathers did eat manna, and are dead: he that eateth of this bread shall live for ever." (John 6: 47 - 58)

Matthew 6: 26-29, is the Biblical basis of the Sacrament of Communion: *"And as they were eating, Jesus took bread, and blessed it, and brake it, and gave it to the disciples, and said, Take, eat; this is my body. And he took the cup, and gave thanks, and gave it to them, saying, Drink ye all of it; For this is my blood of the new testament, (new covenant) which is shed for many for the remission of sins. But I say unto you, I will not drink henceforth of this fruit of the vine, until that day when I drink it new with you in my Father's kingdom."* (also Mark 14: 22-25; Luke 22:14 - 20) Luke adds: *"this do in remembrance of me."* Finally: 1 Corinthians 11: 23 - 34

Jesus has made a new covenant with you in His Blood, and as you partake of the communion, all old covenants you and your ancestors made are broken and rendered obsolete and void and powerless! You may even declare this when you take the cup, saying: **"Jesus Christ, I now seal the covenant You made with me in Your Blood by drinking the wine, which Represents Your Blood, and declare**

every old covenant I and my ancestors, even all the way back to Adam, made with the devil, with any religion, with anything or anyone, broken and all effects over my life and over anyone and anything relating to me, destroyed and all that satan has stolen from me, returned to me seven-fold! I declare this, in Jesus' name!" Then drink the wine! And believe it is done.

Now it is important to seek God, and ask Him to guide you to the church He wants you to be part of (1Corinthians 12,13,14;Hebrews 10:24,25), which is a church where the Holy Spirit has full liberty to operate as He wills.(2 Corinthians 3:6,17) This is a church that preaches and practices the Word of God rightly divided (2 Timothy 2:15). This includes total immersion water-baptism of believers (Romans 6:2-4; Colossians 2:11-12); ministering the baptism with the Holy Spirit of the believer with the evidence of speaking in tongues (Mark 16:17,18); ministering healing, ministering deliverance of the demonically oppressed; ministering in every way, the operation of the manifestations of the Spirit in love. It is a church that operates in Scriptural order through present-day apostles, prophets, evangelists, pastors and teachers, who equippe the believers for the work of the ministry. (Ephesians 4:11-16) Etc. It may be that you cannot find a church that fulfils all these requirements (yet). Then simply go where God sends you. And stay there until it is God; not you yourself, who directs you elsewhere. So many miss God, because they leave a church, for all kinds of reasons. Only if there is heresy, and un-biblical operations, are you released to move, and "come out from among them." (2 Corinthians 6: 11- 7: 1) God knows your heart! Otherwise, be faithful where God directs you, until it is God who moves you.

Now there are services you can watch on the Internet or satellite. This is great if you do not know any other believers, or if church-services are forbidden by totalitarian dictatorships, like Saudi-Arabia! But you múst allow the Lord to guide you to fellowship with other believers. They need whatever contribution God wants to give them through you, and you need them!

You can find Bible-verses in many version and languages, including Arabic here:

http://www.biblegateway.com/passage/?book_id=50&chapter=6&versi
on=9&context=chapter

The Bible in Arabic (probably unfortunately employing the word 'allah'
for God, which you now know is wrong!) can be found here:
http://www.arabicbible.com/

EXTREMELY IMPORTANT – VITALLY IMPORTANT- is that you,
as new believers in Jesus Christ, REMOVE the Old Foundation of your
life and REPLACE IT with a good, solid, Biblically sound New
Foundation in Christ Jesus. (Romans 12:1,2)

The reason that so many ex-muslims fall back into (at least outwardly)
acting like a muslim, is because of the enormous pressures from family
and society, especially if they feel isolated and alone. But most of all,
this is due to not having removed the old foundation of islam from their
lives and not having it replaced with the new foundation in Jesus
Christ!

This is not only so for ex-muslims; this is so for ex-homosexuals, ex-
drug-addicts, ex-Roman Catholics, ex- you name it!

One very good tool is the *Self Study Bible Course* by Derek Prince.

Chapter Sixteen

Be Aware: common words, different meaning

Because the same words often mean different things to muslims and Westerners, it is important that Westerners know what muslims mean by certain words. If Westerners want to communicate with muslims, it is wrong to assume that muslims mean the same thing as they.

To prevent frustrations, and a break-down in communication, and to communicate what the Westerner wants to communicate to the muslim, it is important that the Westerners know the meaning of certain terms to muslims. Democracy has a different meaning for muslims than the western understanding of it.

The word peace has a different connotation, for peace in islam can only be with other countries with islam rule, the *"daar al-islam"* , the house of islam, while with the area's that still have to be conquered, the "*daar al-harb* " , the house of war, no lasting peace can be maintained. *The use of these two terms already clearly reveals the nonsense that Islam is fundamentally tolerant, as the West is boldly and unchallenged being told in their media by muslims, Arabists and related disciplines.*

The Arabic word 'hudna' that Westerners understand as meaning treaty, actually means 'cease fire.' So the Oslo 'peace-accord,' is actually only a cease fire which muslims employ to gather strength to prepare the next attack when they feel ready for it.

Anyone who challenges this, like I do, is not given a voice in the western media, because they have chosen prejudicially, the road of false 'peace', of avoiding all conflict even at the expense of truth!, because of their humanistic views, embracing and stimulating a dialogue between the wolves of islam and the sheep! How blind can the media, the Western politicians, the liberal so called christians, etc. choose to be?

The use of these two terms shows islam declaring war to the non-islamic world; a war with real weapons (often provided by Western

108

weapon-manufacturers), and real killing; a war that will not end until al the world is made part of the daar-al-islam, by force, with the use of the literal sword.

Terms like "freedom of religion" have a total different meaning in Islam than for people with a Western culture, for in Islam it means no more than that Jews and Christian in Islamic countries are suffered as 'dhimmi' citizens, and not forced to convert to Islam (though the social pressures, the extra 'djizja' taxation, and the humiliation are strong factors pushing them towards accepting islam). In that it is fair to say that islam and countries of islam know no freedom of religion.
The freedom in the West to freely discuss one another's religion, and to proclaim it from the housetops, trying to persuade others and win them over, by all means possible and available, is unheard of in islamic countries.

Islam (ab-)uses this freedom in the West to continually attack Christianity, to build mosques everywhere, to publish freely all they want to publish, often attacking Christianity and the conditions in their host-nations etc. freely; while denying and having denied since the seventh century A.D. such freedoms in their islamic nations to the Christians and Jews!

And since Islam is not just a 'state-church,' so to speak, but a 'church-state,' it will never rest until it has gained all control over all areas of life, totalitarian. Already muslims in Great-Britain are calling for separate legislation.

How about all the guest-labourers in Saudi-Arabia doing the same? That would be unheard of in Islamic ears; and Saudi-Arabia even has a religious police force that forces themselves even into homes of foreign workers to see if they have a Bible- study or prayer-meeting, arresting the participants when they do! Let alone that they would allow even one church building on their soil! Yet, this is a nation that Western soldiers fought and risked their lives for; to consolidate such totalitarian dictatorship... I thought Western soldiers only fought for freedom?!? How corrupt can the Western politicians, governments, media, etc. etc. get?

"The Christian should never suppose that words used in common mean the same to the muslim as to the Christian.

"*Sin* " (khatiyya), to the muslim does not indicate something evil in itself. It is only what Allah has declared to be *haram* (unlawful); it may be an evil act in certain circumstances and good in others, for example what he calls a "white lie".

"*Faith* " ('iman): What is intended by this word is the acceptance of the *Shahada* (the muslim confession of faith). So *every* muslim is a "believer" (mu'min)! A person becomes a muslim by quoting, reciting, the confession that "there is no god but 'the-god' Allah, and that Mohammed is his prophet." That is all! He does not een have to believe it! Only speak it once! Satan does not need much to come in!

"*Salat*" (salat-lit.=ritual prayer). The 'salat' is an islamic rite and ritual, that has nothing to do with a prayer from the heart and mind. The muslim prostrates himself 5 times a day in the direction of Mecca (in the beginning of Islam, Mohammed had them prostrate in the direction of Jerusalem, but when the Jews rejected him as a prophet, the direction of the salat, the qibla, was changed towards Mecca. This is another example of Allah changing a verse and regulation in the Koran and replacing it with another), while reciting names of Allah and other islamic confessions, as the playing of a recording. Because the salat is in Arabic the non-Arabic muslims, who do not speak nor understand Arabic, do not even know what they are saying in the salat! That is som e 80 - 86% of all the muslims in the world!

"*Revelation* " (wahy). This word indicates the revelation of Allah by means of the angel Gabriel. It is therefore advisable to use the word 'iclan' for revelation in the Biblical sense, in the contact with muslims.

"*Garden* " (janna) This is not a temporal place but a heavenly land. "Heaven" and the Garden of Eden are synonymous to the muslim. The *fall* of Adam was actually a fall from heaven to earth, that is, a physical fall, not a spiritual or moral one.

The expression "Kingdom of heaven" (malakut assamawat) signifies to the muslim the celestial bodies (*aflak* , i.e. stars).

110

The word "*firdaus* " (Paradise) is the nearest expression if we want the muslim to understand what we mean by "heaven".

There are some expressions which the muslim will not understand at all. If the servant of the Lord uses them, he must be sure to explain what he means. "*The blood of Christ* ". Since the muslim understands by this expression the physical blood of Christ, he would not understand, "They washed their clothes and made them white in the blood of the Lamb". (Revelation 7:14)

The expression "*the New Birth* " perplexes the muslim as it perplexed Nicodemus, but nevertheless, when you express its true meaning, it can be a message of life to him.

The expression "*the filling of the Holy Spirit* " (a;-'imtila' min ar-ruh al-quds) has no meaning to the muslim since he does not consider "the Holy Spirit" to be God but rather the angel of revelation, Gibriel, or even Mohammed, as muslims/islam seek to justify Mohammed's appearance from the Bible, by identifying him with the promised Holy Spirit, as if Jesus was foretelling and promising the coming of Mohammed, thus even making themselves guilty of blasphemy against the Holy Spirit! (Mark 3:29;John 14:16,17;John 16:13-15)

The words "*regeneration* " (tajdid), "*sanctification* " (taqdis), "*justification"* (tabrir) and similar words do not bear the Christian meaning for the muslim whereas the words "*fidya* " (ransom, redemption) and "*kaffara* " (propitiation, atonement) are both understood.

One metaphorical expression popular among Christians should, *never* be used, even with an explanation, namely "Come and kneel at the foot of the cross", and the like. Since the muslim will inevitably take this literally and not spiritually, such an invitation would only strengthen the generally held conviction that all Christians are "cross-worshippers". (Quoted from "Reaching muslims today", a short handbook compiled by North Africa Mission, which itself quoted it from "Why Witness and How".)

Appendix

Recommended Links for More Information on the Internet

Due to the fast-changing nature of the Internet, and the fact that lawmakers seek to gain control over the Internet by abusing their power to make and enforce (evil) laws, as more and more of our world is brought under greater control of governments seeking control even over the minds of the people they seek to enslave more and more under the guise of anti-terrorist measures or protecting the environment etc. – as they are aware that knowledge empowers people and Truth Enlightens and Liberates People, and the ever-increasing Internet-Jihad causing youtube to ban videos muslims complain about, this information is up to date at the moment, but may change at any time.

PRAY! That God will not allow the forces of hell that seek to enslave and murder 5,5 BILLION people of this planet (seek google for information on "The Georgian Guide Stones") to succeed.

PRAY the prayer Jesus taught His disciples: *"Our Father which art in heaven, Hallowed be thy name. Thy kingdom come. Thy will be done in earth, as it is in heaven. Give us this day our daily bread. And forgive us our debts, as we forgive our debtors. And lead us not into temptation, but deliver us from evil: For thine is the kingdom, and the power, and the glory, for ever. Amen".* (Matthew 6: 9 – 13)

For testimonies of ex-muslims go to: http://www.youtube.com/muslims4jesus

For more information about Christianity and Islam:
http://www.answering-islam.org

A good starting point is also http://www.usawakeup.org Dó watch the introduction video. The site opens with links to many very informative sites

Videos:
Quran is not from God. Why?: http://www.youtube.com/watch?v=zMi0v7PdDys

Islam: Why We Want to Kill You – Interview of Walid Shoebat (Palestinian ex-terrorist and ex-muslim) -
Part 1: http://www.youtube.com/watch?v=7Fvot4Xoyno
Part 2: http://www.youtube.com/watch?v=HzLT9wV0l8o

Coptic Priest: **Islam and Christianity**
Part 1: http://www.youtube.com/watch?v=2iLAH9D18-o
Part 2: http://www.youtube.com/watch?v=xx0VzN20mH0
Part 3: http://www.youtube.com/watch?v=AsN7s3Uqw1g

Muslim Clerics leave Islam and embrace Christ by the thousands!:
http://www.youtube.com/watch?v=19FU7Yyx4D4

Father Zakaria: **Jesus Christ is GOD**
Part 1: http://www.youtube.com/watch?v=rBCEnHOn1gI
Part 2: http://www.youtube.com/watch?v=o66lPcPlBZI
Part 3: http://www.youtube.com/watch?v=LOcG1G-52ng

Quranic Verses Inspired by Satan (arabic)
http://www.youtube.com/watch?v=6quHy6rafZ4
Grammatical Errors in the Quran (arabic)- Part 1
http://www.youtube.com/watch?v=g6QVcWWJJIQ
Grammatical Errors in the Quran (arabic)- Part 2
http://www.youtube.com/watch?v=f_s0J7Jlhzk
Sources of the Quran: Al Sahaba _1 (Arabic)
http://www.youtube.com/watch?v=8ABZsZTfDUg
Sources of the Quran: Al Sahaba _2 (Arabic)
http://www.youtube.com/watch?v=xPTLKr3_ods
Terrorism in the Quran-(Arabic)
http://www.youtube.com/watch?v=uKaRSAzzbFE

The disasters of the Quran 1 http://www.youtube.com/watch?v=XYRxrE3-F8U
The disasters of the Quran 2 http://www.youtube.com/watch?v=aM5c2_9Sb6M
The disasters of the Quran 3 http://www.youtube.com/watch?v=XwBZSLmUpgE

Danish Cartoons Zakaria Boutros 1 http://www.youtube.com/watch?v=tULNyfvfq04
Danish Cartoons Zakaria Boutros 2 http://www.youtube.com/watch?v=1erYUFqmyrI
Danish Cartoons Zakaria Boutros 3 http://www.youtube.com/watch?v=3UlMvr4PeTc

John Hagee and Walid Shoebat: Islam Unveiled - Part 1
http://www.youtube.com/watch?v=-e2BD5LDmDE
John Hagee and Walid Shoebat: Islam Unveiled - Part 2
http://www.youtube.com/watch?v=67NScppwC2M
John Hagee and Walid Shoebat: Islam Unveiled - Part 3
http://www.youtube.com/watch?v=YA8lippm9gM
John Hagee and Walid Shoebat: Islam Unveiled - Part 4
http://www.youtube.com/watch?v=1Pna-Z7roxg
John Hagee and Walid Shoebat: Islam Unveiled - Part 5
http://www.youtube.com/watch?v=4Y4hxmf-zWU
John Hagee and Walid Shoebat: Islam Unveiled - Part 6
http://www.youtube.com/watch?v=CMe3gF4CzVY

John Hagee: Who is Allah - is Islam Our Sister Faith? (1/4)
http://www.youtube.com/watch?v=0_bcyqu52a4
John Hagee: Who is Allah - is Islam Our Sister Faith? (2/4)
http://www.youtube.com/watch?v=J1ibvGt7nNg
John Hagee: Who is Allah - is Islam Our Sister Faith? (3/4)
http://www.youtube.com/watch?v=jg-FlCIvWgk
John Hagee: Who is Allah - is Islam Our Sister Faith? (4/4)
http://www.youtube.com/watch?v=i79CMez15wo

The website of father Zakharias Boutros: : http://www.islam-christianity.net/

And: http://www.islameyat.com/

Videos of Ritter1001: http://www.youtube.com/user/Ritter1001

Wafa Sultan speaks up:
http://www.youtube.com/watch?v=2WLoasfOLpQ
Wafa Sultan-Terrorism and Islam (New) :
http://www.youtube.com/watch?v=lYB4pG3kHIY
Warning to West on "Evil of Islam" - Wafa Sultan
http://www.youtube.com/watch?v=gruIHLIH7qs
The Violent Oppression of Women in Islam - Wafa Sultan
(1/2) http://www.youtube.com/watch?v=9_-o7JMVKek
The Violent Oppression of Women in Islam - Wafa Sultan
(2/2) http://www.youtube.com/watch?v=GaSH3tqSMv4
Dr. Wafa Sultan on ISLAM @ UCLA - Mohamed
http://www.youtube.com/watch?v=_JjgHVHKY44
 Arlene Peck interviews Wafa Sultan
http://www.youtube.com/watch?v=haDnKKpI2yU
Wafa Sultan Discusses the Danish Cartoons
http://www.youtube.com/watch?v=q9m-nHGrLdg

What muslims teach:

The Earth Is Flat and Much Larger than the Sun:
http://www.youtube.com/watch?v=7F5kYWceTsI
4 Million Brothers of Apes and Pigs:
 http://www.youtube.com/watch?v=aozorPjJS7g
By nature, men desire more than one woman:
 http://www.youtube.com/watch?v=83lgH97EyME
Wife-Beating Is Permitted by Islam in Muslim
Countries http://www.youtube.com/watch?v=GDSflu4Xhbg

Hamas Bunny Threatens to Kill Danes over Muhammad Cartoons
http://www.youtube.com/watch?v=b0U2ce-LmA4
Hamas' Jew-Eating Rabbit Threatens Denmark:
http://www.youtube.com/watch?v=XQaRh6RVKQs
Jew-Eating Jihad Bunny wants to Kill Danes:
http://www.youtube.com/watch?v=9tkvlQkuWpo
Hamas Rabbit eat Jews:
http://www.youtube.com/watch?v=Jm8w7_P8wZ0
Martyred Mouse and Killer Bee Replaced by Jew Eating Bunny:
http://www.youtube.com/watch?v=SUFynQlbqIg
Hamas hate TV - Nahoul's death and a killer rabbit:
http://www.youtube.com/watch?v=-uPEF7pdRD0

Egyptian Imam Sings About Annihilation of Jewish Apes/Pigs http://www.youtube.com/watch?v=da77TBGm6ak

Teaching Children to die for Allah in Palestine &Lebanon
www.youtube.com/watch?v=Em-MnAYiEWk

http://www.youtube.com/watch?v=tI9VRlAeV_I About a mother who abandoned her 1 and 4 year young to blow herself up as Shahid for Allah, believing the lie she would immediately go to 'paradise.' This was an utterly selfish act, as not only she abandoned her children, but also decided to end the life of others! Not to gain a political motive, as the next video shows, but to gain paradise for herself!

Teaching Children to hate- Only Islam does this abuse of their children!
http://www.youtube.com/watch?v=5AiYIhdZcOg

The following are links to video-recordings of the Programme "Dispatches" filmed undercover in mosques in Great Britain. Watch imams preach:*"We muslims have been ordered to do brainwashing"* About women: *"Allah has created the woman deficient,"* and *"If she doesn't were a hjiab, we hit her,"* Living in a multicultural society: *"You have to live like a state within a state until you take over"* About 'holy war" : "The pinnacle, the crest, the summit of islam is jihad"

1: http://www.youtube.com/watch?v=peFQWuk4nuo (1 of 6)
2: http://www.youtube.com/watch?v=MuCLC8kjWCI (2 of 6)
3: http://www.youtube.com/watch?v=x5t5EqWX92k (3 of 6)
4: http://www.youtube.com/watch?v=yMztM0Z7BYE (4 of 6)
5: http://www.youtube.com/watch?v=V4Zv3BUmwqs (5 of 6)
6: http://www.youtube.com/watch?v=KvjvNScmTQA (6 of 6)

Robert Spencer on islam: http://www.youtube.com/watch?v=SddesLgxzHM &
http://www.youtube.com/watch?v=Q3wyF__kt_w
Robert Spencer - The Politically Incorrect Guide to Islam:
http://www.youtube.com/watch?v=t1Ke7nnedWM
Robert Spencer on The Factor: http://www.youtube.com/watch?v=z9V2IItfu6A
Robert Spencer On the Muslim Veil
http://www.youtube.com/watch?v=trevOrKGBVI

Gbriel Lebanese Anti-Islamic Hizbulla - Ex Islamic:
http://www.youtube.com/watch?v=YTcMBdVeySk

Mohammad Cartoons and Muslim Islamic Outrage:
http://www.youtube.com/watch?v=bd2VEBE-qX8

http://www.youtube.com/watch?v=_X47eBqTls4   Islam - Spread By The Sword
http://www.youtube.com/watch?v=SikIs4qNBPo   Islam - Spread By The Sword 2
http://www.youtube.com/watch?v=8-xqLnxa9BY   Islam - Spread By The Sword 3

http://www.youtube.com/watch?v=yxSjNpMZ-D0   Islam - House of War 1
http://www.youtube.com/watch?v=u0jP-P6ZYYE   Islam - House of War 2
http://www.youtube.com/watch?v=_SXRhY8dWz4   Islam - House of War 3

http://www.youtube.com/watch?v=k-hA59eiySI   Islam - War Is Deceit 1
http://www.youtube.com/watch?v=eHZMA3Ut7q8   Islam - War Is Deceit 2

http://www.youtube.com/watch?v=1-o4l7Mgj5s   Islam - Mandates Violence
Against Unbelievers (part 1)
http://www.youtube.com/watch?v=pV4nemgNNK4   Islam - Mandates Violence
Against Unbelievers (part 2)

http://www.youtube.com/watch?v=mnkBifFRGSA   Islam - Teaches to become a
martyr for islam.

http://www.youtube.com/watch?v=olHVvZQqBT8   Islam: Jihad in the West 1
http://www.youtube.com/watch?v=FWtlPMTzWZA   Islam: Jihad in the West 2

http://www.youtube.com/watch?v=w91MgE3mi80   Jihad On The West
http://www.youtube.com/watch?v=PaCjIdVia1M   CNN, The Latest Terrorist
Tool in the War Against the West
http://www.youtube.com/watch?v=d51poygEXYU   Hitler, The Mufti Of
Jerusalem And Modern Islamo Nazism - in Geman - with English translation
http://www.youtube.com/watch?v=fS81ot0UXN4   Adolph Hitler Meets with
Arab Muslim Grand Mufti Amin Al Hus

http://www.youtube.com/watch?v=rPTioW1LPh8   "Annihilation of U.S
Islam'll take over the world" 1
http://www.youtube.com/watch?v=cip_opNNTbY   "Annihilation of U.S
Islam'll take over the world" 2

http://www.youtube.com/watch?v=yyzjwcQI4hM   Islam- Not a religion of
personal use.
http://www.youtube.com/watch?v=sdnX1YyVMA4   Islam- Not a religion of
personal use.

http://www.youtube.com/watch?v=HAq9PpCUgYU   An Islamic Dr. in London
Justifies Slaughtering
http://www.youtube.com/watch?v=40VFcJTIduw   Iranian Scholar: Tom &
Jerry is a Jewish Conspiracy
http://www.youtube.com/watch?v=DYpR1dLV8L4   Saudi Author Expresses
his opinion on Westerners
http://www.youtube.com/watch?v=8EYRot8ZMpo   Danish Sheik: Europe
Needs Islam

Great-Britain:
http://www.youtube.com/watch?v=rVgRytJFYb4   CNN documentary "The
war within" - 1
http://www.youtube.com/watch?v=EUwa2BR-LJs   CNN documentary "The
war within" - 2

http://www.youtube.com/watch?v=6pDu4YS5To0   British muslims.... their
loyalty is to islam, not to Great-Britain

Palestinian Sheik: "Islam Will Rule U.S/U.K, Jews Are AIDS"
http://www.youtube.com/watch?v=gGpJC3f3UHk

This Book was published earlier in Nigeria - ISBN: 978-31299 - 9

Titled   *"Are Allah and God the Same One God?"*

Made in the USA
Lexington, KY
25 February 2011